LYME REGIS PAST

JOHN LELLO

First published in 1999 by
Lello Publishing
Holmbush, Coram Avenue, Lyme Regis,
Dorset DT7 3LB

ISBN 0 9535164 0 7

Printed by Blackmore Ltd., Longmead, Shaftesbury, Dorset

To Sandra, past, present and future

Previous publications

The Official View of Education, Pergamon 1964

'The Techniques of Teaching' (ed ADC Peterson), Pergamon 1965

Accountability in Education, Ward Lock 1979

Boarding Education in India, Boarding Schools' Association 1989

A Centenary History of Sexey's School Bruton 1991

Accountability in Practice, Cassell 1993

ACKNOWLEDGEMENTS

Anthony Tibbs has edited the script and I am grateful to him. His accuracy as well as his honesty have been invaluable.

I must also pay sincere tribute to the Curator and staff at the Philpot Museum. It is a treasure house filled with helpful and supportive people. I also want to thank warmly the following who have given freely of their knowledge and time. I hope the book does them justice.

Raff Bint
Martine Blanc-Montmayeur
Liz-Anne Bowden
Eileen Broad
Winifred Broom
Albert Brown
John Cable
Anne Case
David Cozens
Alan Edwards
Ernest Evans
Michael Fairley
Pamela Forsythe
John Fowles
Milly Frost
Ken Gollop

Janet Meade (née Wiscombe)
Dennis Mills
Pam Moseley
Sir David Mostyn
Tony Olsen
Alex Orme
Mark Read
Geoff Rowe
Margaret Shaw
Gerald Silverlock
Ted Street
Cecil Symonds
James Taylor
Chris Tozer
Joan Walker
Mary Wilkinson

'Though I milked the cows, the butter I churned is my own' (Charles Lamb)

ILLUSTRATIONS

'Block One'
Plan of Lyme Regis 1841
OS Map of Dorset 1862-8
Earliest Tudor map of Lyme
Town Map 1825
Poor Rate 1681
Family Tree of the Montagu Douglas Scotts
Roman Villa
Roman Head
Thomas Coram
Admiral de Tourville
Facsimile of *Domesday*

'Block Two'
The Gin Shop on the Cobb, the former ammunition store
Staircase in the Tudor House made from a ship's mast
Town Stocks now in the Philpot Museum
Victorian advert for the Lyme stone industry
The cement works on Monmouth Beach
Gravestone of Mary Anning
Mary Anning
William Pinney, MP for Lyme under the Reform Act 1832
CSM Britton

The Muster Roll of the First Company, Dorset Artillery, Lyme 7
The Pilot Boat 1890
Silver Street
Fulling Tower
Broad Street about 1900
A walking funeral pre-1913
Broad Street before 1889

'Block Three'
Extract from the log of the *Ceres*
Granny's Teeth
Steamer coming into Lyme
Marine Walk 1870 showing the cart track from the Cobb to Cobb Gate
The Customs House at the Cobb
Bathing caravans 1870
The Cobb 1890
Lyme Regis Railway Station 1903, about the time of the opening
The Cobb, early 1900s
Air-Sea Rescue launch
SS *Victoria* which plied between Weymouth and Torquay
Shipping on the Cobb 1852
HMS *Formidable*
Part of the funeral of those who perished on HMS *Formidable*
Masterman Hardy, the last sailing boat

'Block Four'
Whistler's studio in Broad Street
The Smith with Sam Govier, featured in Whistler's painting
Victoria Hotel, the railway hotel

Three houses: Alice in Wonderland Café, Wings, Cobb Cliff: all demolished
Late Victorian advert for the Red Lion
St Michael's Church School 1892
Infants 1926
RC Church of St George
Wesleyan Methodist Chapel 1904
Cannington Viaduct 1959 with engines 30582 and 30583
Part of the programme for the opening of the Regent Cinema 11 October 1937
Landslip 1962
A meet at Hunters Lodge 1899
A national tribute to R. Wiscombe
A pigeon from the Wiscombe loft

The line drawings by Sandra Lello

PREFACE

This book covers the main parts of the history of Lyme Regis. It has however been deliberately selective and is not meant to be a comprehensive compendium of all the known facts.

Much of the story is placed in a national context. In some areas this has proved difficult. In others the approach has been rejected where it would have seemed unacceptably contrived.

The greatest problem has been to strive for an appropriate balance and sense of proportion and this has not been possible when significant evidence has been unavailable.

CONTENTS

1 Chapter 1 Physical (and man's relationship to the land)
8 Chapter 2 History
36 Chapter 3 Transport and Communications
44 Chapter 4 Local Trade
51 Chapter 5 Religion
59 Chapter 6 Poverty and Health
67 Chapter 7 Education
77 Chapter 8 Writers, Artists and Designers
87 Chapter 9 Merchant Adventurers
92 Chapter 10 The Defence of the Town
105 Endnotes
109 Primary Sources
112 Bibliography
115 Index

CHAPTER ONE

PHYSICAL

and man's relationship to the land

The geography of Lyme is the key to its past. This scalloped landscape contains the blue clay which hides the fossil evidence of a very distant past. Within the shape of the land directly curved, with ample height and next to the sea, lies the natural shape of a harbour formed by a rocky outcrop. Upon this outcrop, from medieval to modern times, successive walls and sea defences have been built to form a safe anchorage and which today is called the Cobb. Climatically the position of the surrounding hills makes the weather distinctive, and the tilt of the land also has a moderating influence. Immediately to the west the land is called the landslip, and it has fractured in a striking way. This has resulted in the creation of a wild and cut-off area which is different again from the rest of the bay.

But geography is not only about geomorphology, geology and climate: it also concerns the human, economic, and political inheritance of the area. The man-made Cobb harbour has encouraged fishing, shipbuilding and pleasure sailing. The temperate weather has also helped tourism, and made Lyme a pleasant town for people in their retirement, who have provided a stable basis for the local economy. Lyme has drawn other people here to build ships as well as houses, to trade and even start political revolutions, but also to paint, write, rest, dream and build sand castles. The rich paradox is that the nature of much of the local terrain has made large parts of Lyme unstable, yet it is that same terrain which has helped make Lyme geographically attractive and has encouraged the growth of a stable society.

Lyme is fossil rich. The remains of creatures which lived millions of years ago have been preserved by the blue lias clay which contains them. Later they were carried towards the sea when the waterlogged greensand, which lay beneath the lias, moved. Thus the constantly unstable soil both protected and transported the fossil. Even today this volatile soil composition remains. To walk eastwards along cliffs called 'The Spittals', or along the Monmouth Beach to the west, is to walk through a record of time in stone. Fossils of all kinds, but especially ammonites, belemnites and bivalves, are there in profusion, to admire and observe, and they represent forms of life which no longer exist.

The first to explore seriously this treasury was Mary Anning (1799-1847). The daughter of a carpenter in the town, she discovered, in 1828, the first British example of the pterodactyl, that strange and frightening flying lizard. She also found complete skeletons of a 25ft long ichthyosaurus, and a 10ft long plesiosaurus. She led the way in fossil awareness but was soon followed by others for whom the palaeontological profusion in Lyme has made possible many major discoveries.

To appreciate the nature of the coastline it is best to stand at the end of the Cobb and look away from the sea towards the land. From this position it is easy to see the cliffs to the west and to the east, and between them land which is lower and now forms a grassy public park. In this middle part of the Lyme coast, earth slippage is a regular occurrence, but it only becomes threatening when there has been too much rain so that the soil starts to move. In Lyme, this unharnessed power is always present. It is the natural land force and it faces the comparably uncontrolled power of the sea. Lyme is thus set between these two major elements, land and water, and sits as a beautiful jewel in an insecure setting.

An aerial view is equally revealing. It shows how unnatural, in the sense of being artificial, is the position of the Cobb; it reveals the outlying bed of rock on which it is built. It also shows the uneven nature of the land to the west of the town and the equally distorted configuration of the land to the east. It confirms too the need to have a sheltered harbour on this part of the coast. If the Cobb had not been built at Lyme then it would have been necessary to develop Axmouth or to find an alternative harbour. From the air it is also possible to see how the town has developed over the last fifty years. The tightly patterned streets in the centre contrast with the more planned patterns on the outskirts. The older settlements at the heart are much more haphazardly arranged than the more rationally designed layouts on the edge of the town.

As with most towns however, a full appreciation of the layout of the place is best gained by walking round it. Then it is easier to understand that the characteristic hills and slopes provide much of the town's charm and attraction. Cutting through this varied landscape is the River Lym, which was an important source of mill power in the past and is now a vital drain during times of excess rainfall; it comes out into the sea by the new promenade at Cobb Gate. It is revealing during heavy rainfall to walk along the Marine Parade and step carefully across innumerable rivulets. One channel is more substantial than a rivulet and runs down the westward side of the town flowing past the bowling green and into the sea.

The permanent effect of the unstable ground to east and west has been to concentrate building on the land between the cliffs. This has meant that the actual area for development has been relatively small until one is well outside the parish boundary and into the country. Thus the consequences of the local geomorphology have been powerful and impossible to disregard.

Three specific physical features have been of particular importance in their effect on early settlement, and to some extent on current human activity: the place where the river meets the sea, the main communication route on the flat land by the side of the river, and the ever-dominating influence of the sea.

The junction of the river Lym and the sea has always been the heart of the town settlement because it is a natural and human junction. Here the first inhabitants lived, and even today it is the nerve centre of the place. It has currently been chosen as the location for the new sewage scheme, one of the most crucial modern developments; it is also where the most recent addition to the Marine Parade has been built. It is the location of the Guildhall, the Marine Theatre, the Information Centre and the Museum, and is not very far from the Parish Church which has been a place of worship since Norman times. In the eighteenth century the area also contained the Assembly Rooms, at that time the social centre of the town. It was thus an important area from the very beginning of the town story because it was the place where the river water was fresh, the land was flat, and where fish could be caught from the sea. Thereafter, its critical position continued to be important even when it stopped being such a central place for dwellings. It is, and has always been, the core of Lyme Regis.

It is likely that even the word 'Lyme' comes from the nature of the river, for one derivation suggests that it is the Celtic word for 'torrent.' There is another derivation which claims that the word comes from the Greek word for 'salt marsh.' Either derivation would make sense. The river is fast flowing, and it is also the area where salt was first obtained by drying sea water in pans, which was made easier because of the high density of salt in the local sea water.

Hills surround and shut in the town and the only way through them in the early days was to walk or horse ride alongside the river. There it was flatter because the river had cut through the hills and it was easy to follow the river route until you were about two miles from the town. At a much later stage it was possible to cut through the surrounding hills, or build roads over them; but for the earliest inhabitants, the river route was the easiest way to reach the settlement by the sea. Even today there is a path alongside the river Lym which has on either side archaeological evidence of various trades like the textile mills and the water-power mills which used to depend upon the river.

Thus what started as a simple route-way eventually became a larger artery because it was part of the necessary communication for some of the local industries. Gradually the early rough track grew in importance and became a place for people to live as an alternative to being by the sea at Cobb Gate. For many centuries this settlement pattern was the norm until the major routes in and out of the town changed dramatically as soon as wider tracks and roads were cut through the hills or were built over them. This major change of emphasis, however, only really started in the eighteenth century. Until then travelling alongside the river had been the main route-way. It was often quicker to go by sea than to climb out of Lyme and then travel overland.

Of deeper significance was the underlying disadvantage of this slow route because the bucolic river bank was a hidden cause of Lyme's separation from other parts of the region. It is one of the reasons why Lyme was so detached. This made any association with other towns, even local ones, more difficult. It meant that Lyme was also detached in other ways such as in its food supplies and its religious development. Lyme was virtually self-sufficient and it was possible to live there without going outside for food at all. It was also necessary to work out your own spiritual salvation. New ideas were acceptable provided that they allowed inhabitants a high degree of independence. For all these reasons, the river was intrinsic to the development of the early settlement of Lyme.

Even more important was the sea. For Lyme, the sea is not just a feature: it is the justification for the very existence of the town. It remains the most important thing about the place. For the original inhabitants it was the principal source of food. It was probably the route by which they travelled to get to the fresh water of the river. It was an easy beach on which to land, because there was, and is, a break in the tall cliffs.

It is not known where the earliest settlers came from, but it is almost certain that they travelled from mainland Europe and some probably came from as far as North Africa and other parts of the Mediterranean. It is not easy to find human remains on any tidal shore, and in this area the death of a human would make little impression on the much earlier fossil remains which were laid down and covered with sedimentary deposits and exist in profusion from the Jurassic period. However just a little further inland there have been some undramatic archaeological finds, including an Iron Age mirror. Further inland there are much fuller archaeological discoveries in Lambert's Castle, considered briefly in the opening part of chapter 2 on 'History.' Lyme was also one of the places where the Romans landed and then spread out into the surrounding area.

Nevertheless, the evidence of these early landings is slight, and previous commentators, having exhausted the etymology of the word 'Lyme', have moved as quickly as possible to the elements of town history which are easier to trace. This devalues the importance of the sea which tends to get lost in the vagueness which comes from lack of knowledge of hard facts about local pre-history.

CHAPTER TWO

HISTORY

This small town has been closely associated with many important people of national significance. It has also been the background for several events of national importance, of which the most famous was the landing of the Duke of Monmouth in 1685 when he attempted to seize the throne of England from his uncle, James II. Long before that, however, the town had received several royal charters, the first being in 1284 and then renewed regularly afterwards.

The town has not always been politically independent. It had, for example, the closest association with the Parliamentarians in the middle of the seventeenth century. In the century after that, during the days of total political corruption, the town was divided by the support people gave to two politically contrasting families. In modern times however, the town council has tried to work in its best interests regardless of national party political loyalties.

But whatever the local or national political concerns that have affected the town, the dominant influence has always been the sea. It has not only governed the economic state of the town, it has also been the reason why the town has often been raided or attacked. Until the twentieth century the sea had also been the main way of travelling and hence communicating with other people at home and abroad. It was quicker and easier to go by boat to London than to travel by any other means. The Cobb was Lyme's springboard to the outside world.

But the beginning of the town's history starts long before the Cobb was constructed.

Iron Age

Dorset was part of the territory of the Durotriges. They lived mainly in hillforts like Lambert's Castle which can still be visited between Raymond's Hill and Marshwood, on the road from Lyme to Crewkerne. The tribe was a mixture of the indigenous people and the Bretons who came to trade, then settled and intermarried. They were creative, numerous, prosperous, and strong to defend their settlements from attack. They had their own distinctive coins which were often made of silver. Their pottery, usually burnished and dark brown or black, was good enough to be valued and encouraged by the Romans. The invaders eventually exercised a modest control over them but only after a long period of conquest ending in a crushed rebellion at South Cadbury in Somerset.

Roman

At the time of the first landing by Julius Caesar in 55 BC the Romans did not reach Dorset. It was some time afterwards, in 43 AD, that Claudius sent Aulus Plautius to complete Caesar's campaign. A force of 45,000 landed east of Dorset and consisted of four legions with some auxiliary troops.[1] Only a small number came to Dorset and it became necessary to make a frontier which took the form of a road, as was customary with the Romans. This was the Fosse Way which followed the limestone belt between Lincoln and Seaton with an important extension to Exeter. There was also a road from London which came through Dorchester, Chideock, Morecombe Lake,

Charmouth, Raymond's Hill and on to Axminster and Exeter.

Just outside Lyme at Holcombe, and on the shallow site of an Iron Age fort, is the site of a Roman villa and bathhouse. It is close to the known limits of the Romanized area in the southwest, according to F. J. Haverfield.[2] Within the limits of Roman control, there 'were towns and villages and country houses and farms, a large population and a developed and orderly life.' He continues: the 'towns were small and somewhat few, and the country houses indicate comfort more than wealth. The costlier objects of ordinary use, fine mosaics, precious glass, gold and silver ornaments, occur comparatively seldom.' The Holcombe villa reflected that modest description and the finds included a bronze mirror, a comb, and some nails and shards.

It was first excavated carelessly in 1850 by the Reverend George Tucker who, mistakenly, thought it was a ruined church, and twenty years later by Captain John Sackville Swann, an antiquarian who revealed only part of the site and did not discover the most interesting bathhouse. Nearly 20 years ago, the Ministry of Public Buildings and Works authorised a rescue-dig under the direction of Sheila Pollard. She discovered that much of the site had been spoiled by the two Victorian digs, but fortunately the main physical layout, though damaged, could still be seen. It revealed a bathhouse which was 22 yards long, of an unusual octagonal shape, and placed at the end of a corridor with rooms on either side. There was clear evidence of a supply of hot, cold and tepid water, and the bath itself was lined with mosaic. It was, and is, though now again recovered with turf, a precious remnant of Roman life in the Lyme area. Haverfield's final conclusion provides a fitting comment: 'Here among great woodlands and on damp and chilly clay, there dwelt not merely few civilised Roman Britons, but few occupants of any sort.'

Saxon

Sherborne Lane in Lyme is named after the medieval cathedral church in Sherborne. The monks were given land on the west bank of the Lym, not far from its mouth, in 774 by Cynewulf, King of the West Saxons, and also the right to have salt pans to evaporate the sea water by gentle heating and make salt. Mineral salt was not in effective production until the seventeenth century and so the sea salt was of special value to the monks because they used it to preserve meat, fish and eels. It is a fair conjecture that most of the small population of Saxon Lyme would have been employed as salters and fishermen.

Of greater dramatic significance in this period would have been the local battle of 833 which had involved thousands and is mentioned in the *Anglo-Saxon Chronicle*. The Britons of Cornwall joined an army of marauding Danes in preparation for an invasion of Wessex, and they met and fought the Saxons between Charmouth and Lyme. This was part of the more general struggle which had been going on ever since the Danes had started to plunder and invade England. The more concerted attack on Wessex, rather than the struggle at Charmouth, had begun shortly before the accession of Alfred. After seven years of resistance, Alfred was forced to take refuge with a small band of followers on the Somerset Levels. Strengthened by supporters from Somerset, Wiltshire and Hampshire, he attacked the Danish army at Edington (Ethandun) in Wiltshire, defeated them, and the Treaty of Wedmore was signed in 878. The earlier battle near Lyme should be seen as an important part of the overall struggle against the Danes.

Early Medieval

After the first wave of Danish attacks had been repelled by Alfred there was peace for about a hundred years. Then Canute devastated the area around Poole. However, he established a tight authority and restored order. This order was challenged very soon after his death by the Normans who quickly exerted an even more powerful influence. They have left a detailed analysis in the *Domesday Book* (1086) of the economic state of most of the villages in Dorset and there were three entries under Lyme.

1. William Belet's Possession (the Thane). The same William holds Lime. Alveve held (it) T.R.E. (King Edward) and it paid geld for 1 hide. There is land for 1 plough. There is 1 villein and 1/2 plough and 14 salt workers. There is a mill rendering 39d and 3 acres of meadow. (There is) pasture 4 furlongs long and 1 furlong wide and 1 furlong of wood (and) in length and width. It is worth 60s.
   (thane - Saxon dignitary, geld – tax, hide – measure of land which varied between 60 and 100 acres, villein – lowest order of servants)

FACSIMILE PHOTOSTAT[3]

This manor was held until the reign of Henry III (1216-1272), when the Crown acquired it.

2. (Bishop of Salisbury) holds Lym: it is arable land: one carucate; and has never paid the geld. Fishermen rent it and paid 15 shillings to the monks for the privilege of fishing. There are four acres of meadow. The bishop has one house, yielding 6 pence.
   (carucate – as much land as could be cultivated by one plough in a year)

This was part of the Sherborne Abbey Estate and belonged to Sherborne Abbey until the Dissolution. It was during the Norman period that the Cathedral Church of Sherborne became a monastery.

3. Land of Holy Mary of Glastonbury. This church held Lym in King Edward's time: paying geld for three hides. It is arable land: four carucates. Ulviet rented it and still rents it off the abbot, having two carucates, 9 villeins, 6 bordars, and four acres of land there. The pasture is four furlongs in length and two in breadth: also ten acres of wood. There are 13 saltmen who pay 13 shillings. The whole is worth 40 shillings.
(bordar – person who held a bord, or cottage with land, on condition of serving the lord's table with provisions)

This belonged to the Abbey of Glastonbury and included the Colway Manor of today. It extended to Uplyme and was eventually invested in the Crown.

By the reign of Henry III (1216-1272), Lyme had become a prosperous town. It had been considered an appropriate place for the Queen and her son, who was to become Edward I, to embark for Gascony. The Bailiffs were commanded to impress ships for this purpose, and given power to take them by force if necessary. The town was also given the right in 1271 to hold a fair and a market.

The following reign of Edward I (1272-1307) saw some of the most important developments in the status and corporate position of Lyme. In 1284, Lyme was granted its first Charter, and granted the second in 1285. Of equal significance was the acquisition by Edward of the lands of Glastonbury Abbey, as the result of which Lyme became a royal manor and was then designated Regis. The Charters gave Lyme Regis borough status which conferred several major privileges. Foremost was a voice in Parliament by the return of two burgesses, a right which Lyme retained until the Reform Act of 1832 when the two MPs were reduced to one, and then Lyme finally lost sole representation by the Reform Act of 1867. So for nearly six hundred years Lyme had had its own voice in Parliament.

Lyme had the right to have its own merchant guild to govern the commercial activities of the town which included a market. It had the right to hold its own courts and although the assize court met only once, to convict the Mayor, Gregory Charlemayne, of 'certain illegal acts', the hustings court met weekly or fortnightly. The Charter also allowed exemptions from certain tolls and trading fees. It gave direct access to the Crown. A major symbol of the new prestige was the granting of the Common Seal which included the arms of Edward I and Queen Eleanor. The Charter stated that any stranger coming to live and trade in the borough had to become a freeman, or pay 3/6 a week towards the running expenses of the Cobb and sea walls. These were all powerful privileges in the thirteenth century, and the esteem in which Lyme Regis was held can be measured by the fact that the King made a royal visit in 1297.

Edward II (1307-1327) sent an order to the Mayor and Bailiffs ordering them to search for letters which might have come from Queen Isabella whom he suspected of treason. Edward was right to be so careful as it was during the time when Isabella was out to dethrone him because of his fondness for Hugh le Despenser the Younger. Edward lost the struggle, was forced to resign and was murdered in Berkeley Castle.

When Edward's eldest son, Edward III (1327-1377), took over there were other and equally major concerns to deal with. The first was the necessity to rebuild the Cobb which, being made only of timber and rocks, had suffered sea damage. The King gave the town the right to collect a penny from every pound of salt, or from any other goods leaving or entering Lyme. The tax was to be collected for five years which was extended by a further three years. The permanent usefulness and value of the Cobb was thus clearly established by obtaining such financial approval from the King.

The King also ordered two of 'the better mariners' to attend Parliament to consult on coastal safety and on protection against invasion. The context of these precautionary measures was the Hundred Years War with France. Severe damage had been suffered in Lyme as well as in Poole and Melcombe during various sporadic raids, especially in 1377. It was feared that they were the rehearsal for a major French invasion. This did not happen, but during the whole of this time the coastal towns were on constant alert and none more so than Lyme Regis.

Edward III also granted what was called a fee-farm for an annual rent of 32 marks which gave the town certain rights, including being able to charge rents for market stalls and houses, and a toll on all items brought into the town for sale. But a storm at Martinmas, 11 November 1372, ruined the Cobb and therefore Lyme had no safe haven from the sea nor any springboard into it, and the rent could not be paid. Consequently the King was asked to take the town into his own charge and waive the fee-farm arrears.

The Black Death came in several infectious waves between 1347 and 1358. It was called bubonic from the Greek word 'bubo' meaning 'groin' because this is one of the places where there was often a tell-tale swelling; the others were armpit, neck, or any other membranes adjacent to the lymph glands to which the disease was attracted; the incubation period was between two and eight days. It was carried by the black rat (Rattus rattus) and the rat flea (Xenopsylla cheopsis). The death rate was in the order of 40%, so when it arrived at several towns on the Dorset coast, like Melcombe Regis (now part of Weymouth) and Lyme, the effect was devastating. The Plague fanned inwards from the ports, and slowly, but effectively, covered the whole country. But Lyme was one of the places where it first took hold and it hit the local population with powerful virulence. The King, Edward III, stopped any person leaving the town, even a messenger or merchant. Psychologically this must have intensified the demoralising effect of the scourge because one could not get help from outside. But the harsh truth was that there was little anybody could have done which would have been of any use anyway. One could only nurse the afflicted and watch as they died.

The Hundred Years War

In 1377, the year of Richard II's accession, the French Admiral, Jean de Vienne, raided both the port and the town of Lyme, and inflicted heavy damage. It was part of the struggle between England and France in the Hundred Years War. This had begun in the earlier years of Edward III's reign and at first England had been successful and France had agreed to accept the English claim to south-western France. Towards the end of Edward's reign, however, and certainly during the reign of Richard II, England lost the initiative in the fighting. It was at this time that Lyme was occasionally attacked from the sea. This was not only disturbing to the local inhabitants who were being harassed, but it was also a serious obstacle to any trade, especially with France, and a threat to both the stability and the prosperity of the town. However, this was not a time for Lyme to be too self-righteous because the town had provided four ships and 62 sailors for the

Siege of Calais in 1347 and was quite capable of attacking French ports at random. Nevertheless, even if the French attack could have been partly justified as a reprisal for similar attacks by the English, the damage inflicted was considerable and consisted of 77 tenements laid waste or washed away, 71 tenements left empty, 15 ships destroyed and 40 smaller ships damaged and also led to a bill for £300 to repair the Cobb. Richard II took 12 years to reply. During this time there was a constant fear that the French would attack and although the number of occasions that this happened was small, the dread was always present. There was a petition in 1403 which was a concrete expression of this terror and actually mentioned the fear of French invasion as well as the poor state of the town. Only when Henry V had finally brought the Hundred Years War to a conclusion was Lyme Bay at peace again, but it was only a respite before an even more serious challenge came from Spain.

Shipbuilding and seafarers were important to England and Lyme and had been given inducements by the Crown because they were central to the continued life and strength of a maritime nation. Fishing was encouraged as part of that recognition. These incentives helped to pay for imports, trained sailors, increased the number of sailing boats, and were therefore an important foundation of the fleet. To encourage the consumption of fish, specific Acts were passed in 1546 which enforced Fridays and Saturdays as fish days, and these days were extended to include Wednesdays in 1563 during the reign of Elizabeth. Thus there were eventually three fish days a week, to which could be added Ember days and Lent, so that the overall number of fish days amounted to more than half the year. England was thus a fish-eating nation and consequently provided fishermen with secure employment. To enhance their trade even further the fishermen turned to drying and salting fish for export, which presented no local problems for Lyme because the town had been salting fish throughout its history.

Mention 'will be' made of the ships which fought in the Armada, and Lyme's shipbuilding industry was important to the town. The *Revenge*, from Lyme, was a three-master with fore and mainmasts carrying topmasts and square sail, and the mizzen-mast at the stern with a single triangular sail. Matthew Baker (1540-1613) was the designer who worked in conjunction with the practical shipbuilder, but the separation between these two jobs, designing and shipbuilding, was quite new[4]. Several boats were built under this re-organised system in the Lyme yard and they were more sophisticated vessels than had been constructed previously. They had greater manoeuvrability through the use of a tiller attached to the rudder head. Such ships could sail closer to the wind than the heavier Spanish men-of-war.[5] They could also fight at any range and could therefore avoid being boarded. The *Revenge* was a galleon which was to make all existing warships obsolete. It was longer and provided a lower deck on which could be mounted long-range culverins (18 pounders). The upper main deck carried a similar amount of smaller guns like nine pounders and robinets. The fore and aft castles were cut down and replaced by a flat beak-head in the forecastle; the covered after castle housed the officers' quarters and the great cabin. The quarter deck and the open deck were between the mainmast and the mizzen. It was called the *Revenge* because Jack Hawkins, the Treasurer of the Navy, was keen to avenge the attack on the English trading fleet at San Juan de Ulua on the Spanish Main in 1568.

It is clear that Tudor Lyme was a busy place, but it was also constantly threatened by the Spanish navy, and more subtly, by the rapidly changing economic circumstances which were unfolding nationally. England was slowly being affected by national regulations about trade and manufacturing, and this new centrally imposed control was affecting the impoverished and isolated local trades. There was, however, full employment through the successful shipbuilding, fishing and weaving industries. Merrie Lyme was not a romantic fantasy of madrigals and morris men, but a hard-working seaport with vulgar shanties and innovative ship designers, often raided by buccaneers.

A Century of Dissent

Seventeenth-century Lyme was different because it was so stridently political that even religious matters were often embedded in a political context. It was a period of religious dissent because the town chose to separate itself from the communion of the Established Church of England. The word 'dissent' had previously been used to include Roman Catholics, but by this century this connotation was less frequently applicable. Lyme itself supported the Parliamentarians who were Puritans, yet the area was clearly Royalist in sympathy and there were some important Royalist families in the town. It was a confused time. Professor Michael Walzer of Harvard expresses it helpfully. The Puritan insistence on inner discipline was unthinkable 'without the experience of masterlessness. Their object was to find a new master in themselves, a rigid self-control shaping a new personality. Conversion, sainthood, repression, collective discipline, were the answer to the unsettled conditions of society, the way to create a new order through creating new men.'[6] The new Puritan power was not to be taken lightly; the Parliamentary party forced the King to order Popish priests to depart. Consequently, the Reverend Hugh Green went to

The arrival of the Duke of Monmouth on 11 June 1685, with three ships, 1500 suits of armour for the Whig gentry, and between 80 and 150 men, was an attempt to seize the Crown from his uncle James II. Monmouth was the eldest son of Charles II who had died on 8 February in the same year as the landing. He was an important royal. His name was James, a child of Lucy Walters of Haverfordwest in Pembrokeshire and the King. Dr Fuller, Bishop of Lincoln, 'In Verbo Sacerdotis', declared that he had married the couple in secret.[9] James married the Countess of Bauccleuch who was twelve and became James Scott, taking her family name.

Samuel Dassall, the Deputy Searcher of Customs, saw three visiting ships put out seven rowing boats and found that the town cannon could not repel them because all the gunpowder had been used to make fireworks in celebration of the newly received Town Charter. Dressed in purple with large feathers in his hat, Monmouth landed and kissed the soil on what is now known as Monmouth Beach. The Duke's Declaration was then read aloud in which he claimed to be the 'Head and Captain-General of the Protestant forces of the Kingdom.' Dassall left that night to warn the authorities at Exeter and London about the landing, and at the same time the Royalist puppet Mayor, Gregory Alford, rushed to Honiton to report the landing and give the Royalists the chance to organise their opposition. Neither Dassall nor Alford would have had much effect if Monmouth had not delayed his departure by taking three days to recruit. He raised 60 men on the first day and 100 on the second but stayed too long in Lyme and therefore lost the crucial initiative.

The rebels, nicknamed the 'Scythe Men', joined by supporters en route, proclaimed Monmouth King at Taunton on 20 June 1685, and went on to Sedgemoor, near Weston Zoyland, where they were defeated on 5 and 6 July. Those caught were tried for treason under the overall direction of Judge George Jeffreys who was made Lord Chancellor the year afterwards. He came to Lyme himself to ensure that his judicial instructions were strictly carried out.

Twelve men were brought from Dorchester, six in a coach and six in a cart, and then left two hours in an inn at Lyme Regis 'until the butchers had prepared everything for their slaughter. A sledge was prepared to draw them to the place of execution. The horses however would not stir and others were procured who acted the same and so they had to walk to the Cobb to be hung drawn and quartered. The victims were hung in a harness, choked for a few minutes, their clothes were cut off and their bellies split open and their entrails burnt in a fire nearby while the rest of the corpse was quartered and boiled in tar and finally the tar preserved limbs and head were set up along the streets and roads of the district. Two executioners could only deal with twelve bodies a day.'[10]

The twelve who suffered this treatment were Abraham Holmes, Christopher Battiscombe, Benjamin Temple, Arthur Matthews, Joseph Tyler, William Cox, Samuel Robins, Josias Ascue, John Madders, John Kidd, William Hewling and Sampson Larke. William Hewling was executed in Lyme and his brother Benjamin in Taunton. Their sister tried to give a thousand pounds for the bodies of her brothers to be spared from being quartered and exposed but her appeal was denied.[11] Sampson Larke was the first Baptist minister. He was born in Combe Ralegh, Devon, had ministered in London in 1648, and responded to an invitation by churches in Bristol 'to assist them in regulating their congregations' which included Lyme. In 1682 the Mayor carried out a witch-hunt of Baptists so they fled to the fields. But Larke was tough, had been Captain of Horse under Monmouth and there were plans for him to be made a General. 'He was a hard riding

Anabaptist preacher' who with the passing of the years had been made into a hero.[12]

The motives of the insurgents were questionable. Those who supported Monmouth had committed treason, they were trying to overthrow the government. There can be little surprise therefore if the government under such a political challenge took severe steps to deter any who might copy the rebellious followers. Their disloyalty had been as strident as their Protestantism and it had been their well-known anti-Royalist, anti-papist sympathies which had been the reason why Monmouth had chosen to land in Lyme in the first place. The town's support for Monmouth was no temporary gimmick but came from a deeply considered political attitude of the townsfolk. If Monmouth had not been so warmly welcomed the attempted coup would not have lasted as long as it did.

It is also important to remember that Monmouth was himself a monarchist and not a republican. Many of those who supported him had political roots which were often Cromwellian in inspiration. The Calvinist and Anabaptist extremists wanted little Genevas ruled by the tight church 'elect.' Monmouth had no aspirations to being Protector but aimed to be King, and had his rebellion succeeded he would have been as much a king as his father. Monmouth had opposed the Stuarts because they were Catholics but not because they were royal. He believed in monarchy as much as anybody but he wanted a Protestant king and preferably himself. The aims and objectives of many of his enthusiastic followers were more republican.

William of Orange

Because he feared that a rebellion would fail, William of Orange, the Protestant son-in-law of James II, and the Stadholder of the United Provinces, had tried to persuade

Monmouth not to land in Dorset. It is clear, however, that by November 1688 William had changed his mind and that he now saw the British Crown as being within his grasp. He travelled from the Netherlands with a fleet and 10,000 men, and landed some troops in Lyme on the way to disembarking at Brixham in nearby Devon. On this occasion, coming so soon after 1685, many local people, from the gentry to the working classes, decided to stay aloof, mindful of the savage punishments which had been given to the supporters of Monmouth. However, being mainly Protestant and dissenting, the majority in Lyme gave a restrained welcome to William and were relieved to see an end to the Catholic rule of James II.

With the accession of William, England was immediately involved in war with France. The deposed James II, having sought refuge with Louis XIV, controlled naval operations against England from Brest. A French fleet of 110 sailed under the command of Admiral Tourville and was sighted off Portland on 21 July 1690. The French landed and sacked Teignmouth, and by 1 August it looked as though Lyme would be the next coastal town to be attacked. Tourville in his account wrote, 'If the winds allow us to get to Lyme with our galleys it will be very easy to sack and burn that town, which is unfortified and as large as Orleans.'[12] The French had several galleys which were manned by convicts and slaves and each boat carried 150 soldiers. One was seen approaching the Cobb. The 10 sea forts in Lyme, each containing long 9 pounders, opened fire but the galley was too far away. The cannon from the Gun Cliff, however, reached the French boat whereupon she retired and went westward, joined the French fleet and sailed for home. Nevertheless, the threat had been serious and comparable to the challenge of the Spanish fleet in the previous century.

Continuing hostility from France was regularly felt in the threatened invasion from privateers. The Lyme cannon fired against them in 1706 and 1744. Lyme was also ready to repel the French fleet which had promised to support the restoration of Bonny Prince Charlie but this landing never materialised. During most of the French and Napoleonic Wars towards the end of the century, the French had control of the sea until Nelson destroyed their fleet at Aboukir Bay in 1798. By far the most important result of all this maritime tension was that it helped to ruin the previously flourishing trade with France, which had traditionally been a valuable trading neighbour. William of Orange might have been responsible for strengthening the Protestant cause but he was also responsible for cutting off relations with France.

Eighteenth Century

Two families dictated politics at this time: the Fanes, nicknamed the Yellows, and the Coades, nicknamed the Blues. The Fanes were Tory, aristocratic and had their main interests in Bristol. They manipulated the electoral system enabling them to represent the town by buying votes, which they were able to do until after the Reform Act of 1832. The Coades were Whig, Baptist, merchants and from Devon. Both families sought power, or wealth, or both, in Lyme. The Coades were popular because they provided work in the town for woollen traders who were anxious to have their cloth 'finished' in Lyme and then transported to Italy in Lyme ships sailing from the Cobb. They were really escaping from Exeter where the trading competition was fiercer and they had to compete harder to survive. The Fanes only came to the town at election time and did little for the wellbeing of the citizens. Both families used Lyme for their own political or economic advantage at a time when the town was in gradual economic decline.

The blame for the decline is thus only partly to be attached to the indolent MPs because they were in large measure expressing local unwillingness to change. Lyme did not want the kind of leadership, either politically or economically, which was re-shaping other parts of the country, though it is clear, in any case, that the current MPs would not have been able to offer any solution which included manufacturing and offered little to the town other than their infrequent visits. They were not alone in this regard however for nationally the expansion of the country was being led by entrepreneurs, inventors, and creative capitalists. The sleeping giant of English industry was being led not by Parliament and the likes of the Fanes and the Coades, but by hard-working innovators. Lyme missed out on all this because it chose to marginalise itself.

Politically the town was run by bribery, corruption and trickery. The voters of the town consisted of the Mayor and Corporation, the freemen of the town, and the freeholders. In Lyme, as in Weymouth and Melcombe and many other places, the freeholders were men who held freehold land worth forty shillings in any year. It was, however, the freemen who had the effective control in any parliamentary election because they were more numerous, so the Fanes reduced the 120 eligible freemen who had supported Scrope to between 30 and 40 by deviously hiding the Charter, thus having a smaller number to manipulate. The freemen had to be resident in Lyme until 1703, when it was possible to become a freeman by paying. In this way the Fanes got on to the town council in 1733 when the total electorate would have amounted to very few people. But the eighteenth century was corrupt in other ways than in parliamentary elections.

In 1778, Benjamin Follett, Town Clerk 1735-92, and his sons Thomas and John with the support of three mayors, organised a revolt against the Fanes. Their formal complaint, technically called an Article, claimed that the Fanes had 'wilfully absented themselves from Lyme Regis' and 'wilfully omitted and neglected the duty and execution of office which caused great hindrance and delay to the business of the mayor and corporation of the town.'[14] Those who had complained were ousted a month later. Several other and later Articles of Complaint were similarly rejected and the Fanes invariably won the subsequent appeals. There can be no doubt that the Fanes were able to control the contemporary legal and municipal scene in ways that avoided more formal administrative procedures. In short they were permanently corrupt.

England had also become involved in European wars because George I, the imported King from Hanover, had brought mainland problems and conflicts. These wars were the Austrian Succession (1739-48), the Seven Years War (1756-63), and the American War (1775-1783). The Austrian War involved England fighting France, Spain, Prussia and Bavaria. The Seven Years War was against France, Spain, Austria, Russia and Saxony, and the third was against France, Spain, Holland and the insurgent American Colonies. All these wars were European and Colonial and involved the sea. For this reason, Lyme was directly concerned because it was still an important port even though it had declined in importance since 1677 when it had been fourteenth in the whole of England. The biggest threat was from France, a traditional rival which had regularly attacked the south-western coast of Devon and Dorset, but had now become a more formal enemy. The fear that the French buccaneers might maraud, as they had done in the previous century, was always present. In 1795-6, the latest of several Navigation Acts instructed many counties to provide specific numbers of men, and Lyme was instructed to find 23 sailors.

However, life in eighteenth-century Lyme was not only about mercantile decline, naval skirmishes and political corruption. It became a town which was frequented by the famous. This was partly due to Thomas Hollis (1720-1774), writer, scientist, traveller and republican, who had the ear of many important people. He retired to nearby Beaminster, frequently stayed at the Three Cups in Lyme, and was the first person to see the potential of tourism in the town. He bought much land and property, and built the eastern end of the Marine Parade. Because of him, Chatham (1708-1778) came to stay with his son Pitt (1759-1806) who was having a break from Oxford. The influx of influential politicians was also encouraged by Dr Richard Russell who promoted the virtues of sea water. So it was that although Lyme was a corrupt political dead end in the local context, it became one of the national centres of political intrigue and influence because people of distinction took holidays in the resort.

Most of the famous visitors regularly went to the Assembly Rooms. Valerie Grosvenor Myer, in *Obstinate Head, Jane Austen, a Biography*, describes the range of activities: 'Music (was) provided by three violins and a violincello on Tuesdays and Thursdays. The subscription was fifteen shillings and sixpence. Subscribers paid two shillings for balls, and one shilling for card assemblies on other nights. Tea and coffee cost sixpence. Sixpence was charged for cards, chess, backgammon. Everybody else was charged double.'[15] John Fowles in *The French Lieutenant's Woman* also mentions the Assembly Rooms and places them in a Victorian context: 'The place provoked whist, and gentlemen with cigars in their mouths, and balls, and concerts. In short, it encouraged pleasure... When the Assembly Rooms were torn down in Lyme, the heart was torn out of the town; and no one has yet succeeded in putting it back.'[16]

Nineteenth Century

Mary Anning (1799-1847) was following her father Richard's footsteps and collecting fossils, Jane Austen was writing *Persuasion* in 1803-4,[17] streetlighting was introduced in 1836, and the landslip in 1839 endowed Lyme with a permanent nature reserve; and while all these things were happening there was a clean-up in the political life of the town. It began with the passing of the 1832 Reform Act. The number of men who got the vote was only slightly increased and no women were enfranchised until the next century, but the momentum for universal suffrage had begun. There was a major redistribution of parliamentary seats so that the newly developed cities in the north and midlands could receive a more appropriate representation for their increased population. Consequently the two MPs which Lyme had long enjoyed were reduced to one and the first MP to be elected under the new organisation was William Pinney. The effect of increasing the number of voters was to make bribery impossible.

Henry Holt Henley, the Lord of the Manor, had brought an action against the Corporation and alleged that the sea walls had become defective and his land had been flooded. Henley succeeded in this case which was heard in Winchester and was awarded £100; this was increased to £3,041. 10s after an appeal in the House of Lords. It was this court case which led to further investigation in a Public Enquiry in 1833.[18]

This was held on 13/14 December 1833 in the Guildhall under Edward John Dampier. It was called to discuss how Lyme was governed, and by implication was concerned with the actions of the Town Clerk, the Recorder, the Chamberlain, the Coroner and the Cobb Warden. It reported that 'all the members of the Corporation seemed to be members of one family and owe position to the influence of the family.' This changed with the appointment of George Smith, a lawyer from Axminster, as Town Clerk, and it was he who largely ensured that the town was thenceforward run in a less corrupt manner and not dominated by just one family.

Local government was radically changed by the Municipal Reform Act of 1835 and Lyme was one of the 250 municipal corporations which were affected. The Whig government set up a Commission to investigate the facts, and young barristers, called assistant commissioners, visited every municipal borough and found Lyme like some others, corrupt. The old boroughs were formally dissolved and their property, debts and powers were transferred to councils, elected by ratepaying householders of three years' standing. At first little differences could be seen because the old boroughs had done so little, but eventually better organisation and fairer representation slowly made for some improvements in the way towns were run. It was still possible, however, for two Parliamentary Enquiries in the 1840s to reveal corrupt electioneering; in Lyme, as in other parts of the country, Acts of Parliament did not always cure the ill, but at least the problems were now recognised.

The population of Lyme fluctuated considerably during the nineteenth century as the following table from the Victorian County History shows:

1801	1451
1811	1925
1821	2269
1831	2621
1841	2756
1851	2852
1861	2537
1871	2603
1881	2290
1891	2365
1901	2095

These are de facto population figures, which means the resident population at a particular time and not the population really belonging.[19] They have little relationship with the national figures for recession and prosperity:

1832-5	good harvests and full employment
1836	bad harvests and financial crisis
1837	recession and unemployment
1838-9	slight revival
1840	good year
1841	depression
1842	deeper depression
1843-5	revival
1847	financial crisis - railways

(from Asa Briggs *The Age of Improvement*[20])

This general analysis of national boom and bust shows that economic conditions do not seem to have affected Lyme. The railway, for example, came as far as Axminster in 1859, but the branch line did not reach Lyme until 1903. Consequently the trade dependency on the railways left Lyme untouched. Chartism, that mid-nineteenth-century protest by the skilled craftsmen and tradespeople, is another example of a national movement that did not reach Lyme. It came no nearer than Yeovil where there were only seven nominations to the representative General Council. It is fair to claim that during the nineteenth century Lyme slowly and undramatically declared a kind of UDI from the rest of England and, at times, even from Dorset itself. In some ways this isolationism has continued to the present. Lyme did more than cut itself off from national trends in manufacturing and industry, it decided to run an independent economy of its own making. This was a form of evolution while the rest of the country was having an industrial revolution that defiled and enriched at the same time. Economically Lyme had to learn the important truth that to be genuinely independent often meant going against a national trend. It is a lesson the town has not forgotten.

The century ended with two massive celebrations commemorating the Golden Jubilee (1887) and the Diamond Jubilee (1897) of Queen Victoria. There was a parade in front of the Baptist Church, a favourite gathering place in Lyme before the motor car dominated traffic, and there were parties, and services in all the churches, showing a deep enthusiasm and respect for the monarch. These two occasions marked the end of a national lifestyle which was soon to disintegrate.

Twentieth Century

One of the great dramas of the 1914-18 war was the sinking of HMS Formidable which was torpedoed in Lyme Bay. The survivors were landed at Cobb Gate. Some of them were taken to the Pilot Boat inn where the landlord, Mr Tommy Atkins, had a collie who lay beside a man thought to be dead. He licked the man and 'warmed him back to life.' The story reached the national papers and was reputed to be the motivation behind the 'Lassie' dog films made in Hollywood.

The town was exhausted after the war and only slowly recovered from the loss of a generation of young men so poignantly remembered at the war memorial in Monmouth Square. But peace was not to be permanent and one of the ominous, yet revealing indications of insecurity in the town, as well as in the country, came with the formation of the Air-Sea Rescue Service in 1937. It lasted continuously until it was disbanded in 1964.

When the war broke out in 1939, all thoughts of tourism immediately disappeared because the beach was cordoned off for the duration. Out at sea a section of Lyme Bay was a bombing range but it could be used only during daylight hours and not at weekends. The odd enemy bombs were dropped and did not damage because they were mostly dropped in the sea, but the worst moment was the strafing of Coombe Street though fortunately there were no casualties. There was the full range of wartime services like the Home Guard, the Air Raid Precaution Service (ARP), the First Aid Service, the Fire Service (AFS), and the Special Constabulary. They all trained wherever they could, in schools, the village hall, and in places like the Talbot Arms skittle alley. Money for ambulances was quickly and successfully raised. However, the target was not reached during 'Wings for Victory' Week. Fourth time Mayor, W.J. Emmett welcomed the Officers and ship's company of HMS *Lyme Regis* to a reception in the Town Hall on 15 August 1943. They were led at that time by Commander F.G. Tidswell DSC, accompanied by Lt Goff RNR. It was said that throughout the whole of its short history, 1941-48, HMS *Lyme Regis* never had a Lyme-born man on the strength. It did have a distinguished life as a minesweeper and took over the task of sweeping Sword Beach before the D-Day landing when the leading minesweeper HMS *Fraserburgh* was damaged.[22]

One of the busiest times in the history of the town was the accommodation of a very large number of American Servicemen who were billeted prior to the D-Day landings on 6 June 1944. The Marine Theatre was used as their PX, an equivalent to the NAAFI. They sailed for France from Weymouth harbour because it had a deeper draught than the Cobb, but the effect on Lyme of the trade, noise and romance was also a major if rather different kind of invasion from the one in Normandy. Lyme was apparently very quiet again after they had gone.

CHAPTER THREE

TRANSPORT AND COMMUNICATIONS

The town is at the seaward end of a river valley and so is accessible by sea as well as land. It looks both ways, it is approached from both ways, and this open location has always ensured the town is outward looking. The key element in the development and expansion of Lyme is the Cobb because it provided safe anchorage for ships and protection from the south-westerly winds, and so encouraged ships to visit Lyme. The Cobb has been in existence since the reign of Edward III. It opened the town to European trade and competition and much local coastal travel, but also to a great deal of piracy and raiding. Thus it was, at the same time, a boon and blight. The only other routeway into the town for hundreds of years was the packhorse route which connected with the main route to Sherborne, the ecclesiastical centre of the area. The railway, built 60 years after the national railway boom, was always only a branch line of the main line between Exeter and Waterloo. Although as picturesque as toy town, and loved by holiday-makers, the railway never had any significant influence on town commerce. Finally it is important to mention the vital roles of the lifeboat, the wartime Air-Sea Rescue Service, and the coastguards. All three provided a backup for the proper monitoring of travel and work at sea.

Inaccessibility from the land has influenced the character of the town. There were two land routes. One was the packhorse trail which went along Coombe Street following the river and so up the hill and out of town. The other was along the cliff path to Charmouth which no longer exists, because the coastal cliffs have crumbled and part of the path has fallen into the sea, but it was more used than has been popularly supposed because the going was relatively easy. The cliff path to Seaton, even before the landslip, was never free from subsidence, and to travel westwards it was necessary to go up the valley and join the old Roman road to Axminster and thence to Exeter.

Travelling by packhorse was popular throughout the west country until about the last hundred years. It was arduous at the best of times for man and beast because many of the paths were very rough, often got very muddy through over-use, and the horse needed goading and constant encouragement. The animal had boxes, bags or baskets slung from the pack-saddle, and since this was often the main method of cartage the total weight was often heavy. A usual load for a pony was about 125 lbs (57 kg). It was common for the traveller to have one horse for his luggage and one for himself. There were, however, also pack pedlars who went around visiting every cottage without a pony or horse and the average weight for a man to carry was 60 lbs (27 kg).

There was a trackway below the church just wide enough for a horse and cart, and when this was enlarged in 1824 part of the church had to be demolished to make room. This gives some indication of the importance of the road to the town, and, as well, shows a lower priority and respect for the oldest part of the building. Even as this book is being written there is still controversy about the width of this road, the narrowness of the pavements and the traffic congestion.

The road down to the Cobb was too steep to be in common use. It was first mentioned in the town plan of 1841 and was then called the New Road. It has always been liable to subsidence although there are houses along it which have remained standing for over 200 years. Nevertheless the road is very unstable and uneven. For these reasons, the steepness and the instability, most goods and people travelled from the Cobb along the beach at low tide because it was flatter and direct. At the town end of the beach is the Cobb Gate where, during the eighteenth century, there was also a Customs House on the spot where the lavatories are now situated.

The Cobb played a central role. All ships anchored in its lee, and it was there that goods were loaded or unloaded. It was not connected to the land until 1756, so a system of Cobb porters, strictly licensed by the Mayor and Borough, was responsible for carrying goods to and from the Cobb via the Customs House at the Cobb Gate, half a mile distant at the bottom of Broad Street. This carriage of goods across the intervening half mile was achieved by packhorse at low tide, small boats at high. The horses were perfectly accustomed to the operation. Tattersfield quotes an eye-witness account: 'They have no drivers, but are charged with Bales at the Warehouse, and away they trot to the Ship's side, and stand fair, sometimes above the Belly in Water, for the Tackle to discharge them; and then they gallop back to the Warehouse for more. And so they perform the Tide's work, and know by the Flood when their Labour is at an End.'[23]

The reason for stressing in detail the trading routes in and out of the town is to emphasise the important point that Lyme was very cut-off from the rest of the district during most of its history. This tended to make the place inward-looking and almost self-sufficient. In chapter 6 on 'Health', reference is made to the work of Joan Walker, who makes the same point about the town being dominated by a few families. Later in this chapter and elsewhere the work of the RAF Air-Sea Rescue Unit is mentioned, and only recently a Lyme resident observed that the town was enriched by the coming of that Unit because many of the men had stayed on after they were demobilised, had married local girls, and so brought fresh blood to the local population. Although the sea is the town's frame of reference, and its escape route, this does not always remove the isolationism which is more an attitude of mind than a geographical accident. The sailor who goes to work in a trawler does not necessarily achieve anything wider in outlook than just catching fish (especially the renowned Lyme shellfish close to the shore), and for many the net in the sea was as peculiarly local as the plough on the land.

The sea also brings wider perspectives and perceptions from outside the town. For example, the men of Lyme contributed significantly to the navies which were needed in times of crisis during the wars with Spain under the Tudors, and later during the Revolutionary and Napoleonic wars against France. These were much more than windows on the world; Lyme was an important port, and sometimes central to those wars. The threat of invasion from the Spanish Armada, for example, was observed from the cliffs to the east of Lyme by sailors and landlubbers alike and was felt by all the local people, not only those whose lives were jeopardised fighting at sea.

There were also more regular and less critical maritime influences which were not parochial. It was easiest to travel by sea until proper roads were built in the nineteenth century, the sea being a universal thoroughfare. When the nineteenth-century Chartist, William Lovett, first travelled to London from Newlyn, he went by boat and could easily have called at Lyme en route. The whole journey from Cornwall to the capital would have been much quicker by sea than if it had been made by horse or carriage. By the end of the nineteenth century sea transport was extensive and there were regular steamers operating between Lyme and Weymouth by Cosens and Co, and a service between Lyme and Exmouth. Passenger boats regularly called in at Lyme from many parts of the southwest and there were also cargo boats of all kinds which came from all over the world. There is a customs duty list of 1490 listing a wide range of goods which came mainly from Europe and included countries from all over the world; there was trading with the Mediterranean, Africa, the West Indies and the Americas, Russian timber ships, and cod trawlers from Newfoundland.

Piracy involved travel practices which were unorthodox but effective. Most pirates waylaid vessels heavy with goods on the homeward run. St Malo, Morlaix, and the Channel Islands were some of the popular ports used, but everywhere on the English and French coasts had a share of illegal trading. It bore comparison with the black market during the last war and was tolerated because it was often useful.

The smugglers as well as the pirates were very good sailors and could always be recruited in an emergency. They also had the most intimate knowledge of the local ports on both sides of the Channel. It was not surprising that some people of influence and wealth could not resist supporting some of these clandestine activities, and the boundary between the legal and the illegal was often blurred. During the wars with the French, many smugglers were employed as secret agents. One was John Copinger (the Dane), married to a Devon girl, who traded illegally and profitably all along the south coast from Cornwall to Dorset and across to France, and when the French wars broke out acted effectively as an English agent.

Jack Rattenbury, still a family name in the town, was called the 'Rob Roy of the West.' He was the best known local privateer, a general word intended to cover all the illegal acts which happened at sea. He is probably best known because of the publicity which came from his *Memoirs* published in 1837. He was born in Beer, was a fisherman at nine, married a Lyme girl, was a skilful smuggler, a naval pilot, a wily charmer, sometime Revenue collector on the *Tartar* and the *Catherine*, a prisoner and an escapee from prison; he was a colourful character known all along the coast but especially in Lyme and was summoned to the House of Lords to give evidence about the local coast because he knew it so well.

By the middle of the nineteenth century, transport in Lyme was slowly changing from the sailing boat, the pony, and the post chaises (like the 'Defiance' which operated between Lyme and Bridport and started at the Royal Lion), to the passenger-carrying steamer and the horse bus. It was a very gradual transition because the steep hill into town was still a great obstacle. The hill had deterred the horse-drawn coaches from London and discouraged the major carters. Only goods which could be put on a pack-horse could be carried in and out of town. Persistent difficulties over the width of roads and paths into Lyme have always caused transport problems. As to sea transport, even the Cobb does not have a deep enough draught for large ships.

The first turnpike, built in 1759, helped to improve the roads, but it was the coming of the railway to Axminster which eventually gave rise to the horse bus which went to and from Axminster from 1878 onwards. The Lyme Light Railway which was built after the passing of the Light Railway Act of 1896, connected Lyme with the main line at Axminster which went from Exeter to Waterloo. The journey took just over three hours from Axminster to London. Arthur C. Pain was the engineer and had previously been involved with comparable light railways, the Southwold line and later the Culm Valley line. The long awaited opening took place with great ceremony on 24 August 1903. The Mayor with mace bearer was there, with the Vicar resplendent in top hat. This impressive procession walked from the station, behind the marching constabulary and into town. The finances of the railway, however, turned out to be less impressive and eventually the majority shareholder, the London and South Western Railway Company having originally held only 55% of the equity, took over the whole of the railway on 1 January 1907.

One of the major expenses in constructing the track had been the building of the Cannington Viaduct, which was interesting because it was one of the first viaducts in the country to be built in concrete. It spans the southern end of the Uplyme valley and without it the railway could not have been seriously contemplated. The first train went over on 22 January 1903 and the Viaduct was formally opened on 24 August 1903.

When the LSWR took over the railway some changes were made. Signals were installed in 1907, and in 1912 the original lightweight flat-bottomed rail was replaced. On 11 January 1923, the line became part of the Southern Railway, in 1948 part of British Railways Southern Division, and subsequently transferred to the Western Region. Goods services were withdrawn on 3 February 1964, and there was a short period of diesel operation before passenger services were closed down on 28 November 1965.

The Lyme branch line offered six return journeys a day when it opened; this was soon increased to eight, and later settled down to 10 or 12. Much loved by young and old visitors, it was like starting a holiday on a railway from toy town. Sadly, few commuters ever travelled regularly and it was an economic failure for half the year.

Two of the old engines used are still in service. The most famous is the *Lyme Billy*, whose real name was the *Drummond*, which is still used on the Blue Bell Line in Sussex. The *Freshwater*, constructed in 1876 at the Brighton works, was sold to the London and South Western Railway in 1903 for the Lyme branch line. It was eventually acquired by the Isle of Wight Steam Railway where it has been on active service since 1981. The old timber Edwardian station at Lyme was demolished and rebuilt at Alresford near Winchester where it is now part of the Mid-Hants Railway from Alresford to Alton (the Watercress Line).

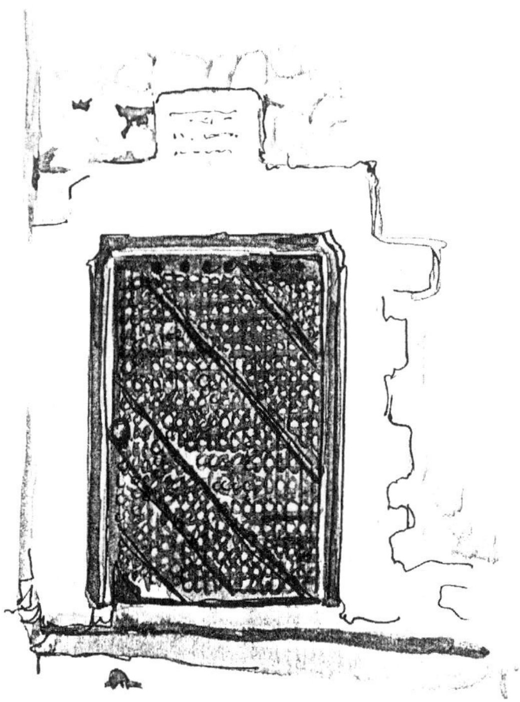

The Old Lockup.

CHAPTER FOUR

LOCAL TRADE

The earliest mention of trade is the supply of salt for the monks of Sherborne in 774. It is most likely that this industry of drying the salt water in open pans had existed for some time beforehand. It is also likely that the same method was used by local people for the purpose of drying fish.[24]

The Romano-Celtic settlement at Holcombe predates the Sherborne trade by over 300 years, since a coin of Constantius II was found which dates the building to between 323 and 337 AD, although the second Roman landing had arrived in 43 AD to complete the much earlier campaign by Julius Caesar. The site at Holcombe revealed a variety of artefacts including a bronze ring, a child's bone spoon, purple beads, and fragments of a brooch; and on an adjacent site a Celtic bronze mirror was found. There is also evidence of growing wheat and rearing cattle.

With the coming of the Normans there was a direct monarchical link with mainland Europe and with it came a wider development of trade, especially with France. The Norman King Edward I especially assisted Lyme by allowing fairs and markets, and by establishing a merchant guild in the second Charter (1285). This organisation greatly helped the trades by giving a simple structure to all commercial activities including a market. His second Charter awarded the town a Seal which, among other features, includes a ship at sea - a royal recognition of

Lyme's important trade of fishing and seafaring. The Charter also stated that any stranger coming to live and trade in the borough had to become a freeman or pay 3 shillings and 6 pence a week towards the running expenses of the Cobb and the sea walls. The repair of the Cobb has been one of the main industries in the history of Lyme ever since.

There has been a succession of industries connected with the sea but the only consistent one has been fishing, which has had a place in the list of town businesses in all ages. Domesday fisheries tenants were obliged to give 15 shillings to the monks in respect of their fish (ad pisces). There are records from all periods of shellfish being caught in the Bay, particularly shrimps, prawns, crabs, scallops and lobster; the smaller of these were caught in the Dorset dorser, a form of pannier. Large numbers of mackerel started to arrive quite unexpectedly in the eighteenth century, having inexplicably left the northeast of the country, and it was common until recently to be able to see glistening shoals of them swimming off the Cobb. Pilchards, slightly smaller than the herring, were also coming in good numbers in 1724 though there are no early records of their being fished. In the nineteenth century, a Shipping Register of 1 March 1869 records that there were 163 certificates issued for small boats which was a large number for a small harbour. Roberts, in his history of Lyme, mentions oare which was an early form of seaweed harvested on rock ledges of which there were approximately 500 acres. In was necessary to have the Mayor's licence to burn this seaweed, and in the reign of Edward VI the Mayor received 27 shillings, and in 1589 received 40 shillings for three years. At the time this book is being written the fishing fleet has shrunk almost to non-existence, but shellfish are still being caught in the Bay and are being sent mainly to the Orient where the prices are high enough to justify the cost of transport.

It was the fame of Lyme fishermen which gave the town its reputation for producing good sailors and it is true that they served in every major sea conflict in the history of this country. During the much earlier reign of Edward III (1327-1377), three ships with 42 mariners had gone to assist in the Siege of Calais. The participation of Lyme in campaigns at sea in Tudor times had also been constant, considerable and important, both in the recruitment of sailors and also for the regular need to provide fighting ships to attack the Spanish. It was much the same story in the wars against France during the Revolution and against Napoleon. But there was a thin line of distinction between fighting for England on the one hand, and being a buccaneer or a pirate on the other.

The second part of the Rattenbury *Memoirs* begins: 'I was engaged ostensibly in the trade of fishing, but, in reality, was principally employed in that of smuggling.' This ambivalence was enjoyed by many other men. Rattenbury was, however, highly respected but this did not prevent him, and his sailing mates, from being smugglers as well. The Confidential Orders Books of a local coastguard suggest that smuggling was continued at an almost professional level until at least 1867, and probably until considerably later.

Shipbuilding continued to be a major industry until ships became too large to get into the Cobb. Then the local boat industry began to decline, although it did continue to serve a more modest but important function for many years maintaining existing craft. The Sea Fisheries Act of 1868 decreed that all boats had to be registered, and the Shipping Register at this time includes eleven ships from Lyme, including a decked trawler of 17 tons.[25] However, after this the shipbuilding industry in Lyme slowly fell away.

While the men were at sea, and a large proportion of the men of Lyme did spend considerable periods away from home, the women worked at weaving wool, working with silk, and making lace. In Lyme these had been important trades over many centuries. The wool came from the sheep farming, the silk was imported, and the lace was one of the traditional occupations for many women in this part of the southwest. In the eighteenth century, weaving broad and narrow cloth was the main industry away from the sea, and Lyme was one of the centres of it in the west country. Lace-making was of comparable significance, and according to the local historian Roberts, Broad Street was 'chiefly inhabited by lacemakers who worked at their doors in the summer;'[26] doorways in other parts of the town like Sherborne Lane would have witnessed the operation of the same craft. The work of these skilful women must have been held in high esteem, because Queen Caroline's lace wedding dress for her marriage to George II in 1727 was made in Lyme. This was during the period when the town was becoming the seaside resort associated with Bath, and the two were as popular as each other with the fashionable element in English society.

In the preface to *Far from the Madding Crowd*, Thomas Hardy comments on how country life is changing, and writes that the 'change at the root of this has been the recent supplanting of the class of stationary cottagers...by a population of more or less migratory labourers.' This comment does not apply to Lyme which had quite a different population pattern. Here many families had husbands who were often absent and wives who stayed at home and were the preservers of continuity through practising a craft as well as running a family. This combination made Lyme stable and different from many other towns.

The many and various textile industries made use of the fast-flowing river which was suitable for driving the mill wheels. The town mill was also used for grinding wheat and is currently being restored; there were other mills alongside the river which have either disappeared or have been converted for different uses. The mills were important in the history of Lyme until the late nineteenth century. At the end of Coombe Street there is a round tower which looks as if it is of Norman origin; it is in fact the remains of a factory built in about 1830 which used a patent process for fulling, or cleansing and thickening cloth, by steaming.

Brewing was well established in the town but is now no longer. The Abbot of Sherborne claimed the assize of beer. The historic Cobb Ale is less old and dates from the destruction of the harbour in 1372. Later references to brewing are colourful and suggest that beer was always a popular beverage. Mr Hooker of Lyme was fined two shillings and sixpence in 1599 for breaking a fast day; it was also forbidden to sell beer during Divine Service. In 1612 it was decreed, 'none to tipple for more than an hour' in one house. Widow Brooks was dismissed in 1653 for brewing and selling ale for divers disorders, and in the same year, Mary Somers was whipped for selling ale without a licence. Throughout the nineteenth century, both ale and porter (bitter beer made from malt) were brewed in the town.

An active coal-importing industry was based on the Cobb with much of it coming from the northeast and Wales. Beatrix Potter illustrated her book 'The Tale of Little Pig Robinson' with drawings of the town and there is a passage about coal ships: 'Near the steps coal was being unloaded from two grimy colliers called the *Mar-*

gery Dawe of Sunderland, and the *Jenny Jones* of Cardiff. Men ran along the planks with wheelbarrows of coal; coal scoops were swung ashore by cranes and emptied with loud thumping and rattling.' It is clear that the Cobb was not always the idyllic place it is now. It was a busy, crowded, active harbour with sailing ships, sailors, fish, timber and coal, and with all kinds of goods lying around.

In the early part of the nineteenth century there was also the important industry of sea-quarrying on the seashore. This was first developed by Henry Henley of Colway Manor, a London Road contractor. He quarried the limestone edges of the foreshore and used it for infill and in the making of stucco. Soon other contractors followed suit, so that before long much of the natural protection against sea erosion had been removed. The tough men who worked in this industry were called the stoneboat men; they carried the quarried stone back to the Cobb where it was often used as ballast for the colliers returning to other parts of Britain.

Tourism eventually took over as the main business of the town. The first serious move in this direction started in the eighteenth century under the leadership of Thomas Hollis (1720-1774). He bought much old property and demolished it, thus opening up many parts of the town. He was also responsible for building the eastern end of the Marine Parade. Then he started to make plans for the Assembly Rooms, and encouraged famous people like the Pitts, Chatham and William Pitt the Younger, to visit Lyme, so linking the town with sophisticated Bath society. From this moment the town was established as a resort and has remained one ever since. Associated with this changed nature was the changing nature of the accommodation in the town. It soon became a favourite place for retired people. They liked the gentle climate, the beautiful views, and the ready supply of cheap labour to do the housework. As tourism slowly grew, so the more traditional trades and crafts began to decline. The understandable attraction of steady money in hotels and boarding houses did great things for the wellbeing of the family, but militated against the continuance of time-honoured, labour-intensive skills like lace-making.

As with most of the southwest, heavy industry never came to Lyme. It was not an ideal location because communications were difficult; roads into the town were narrow, steep, and not always in good repair. There were no natural coal resources. It was also some distance from London and although heavy goods could be sent by sea, and often were, the voyage did take a long time.

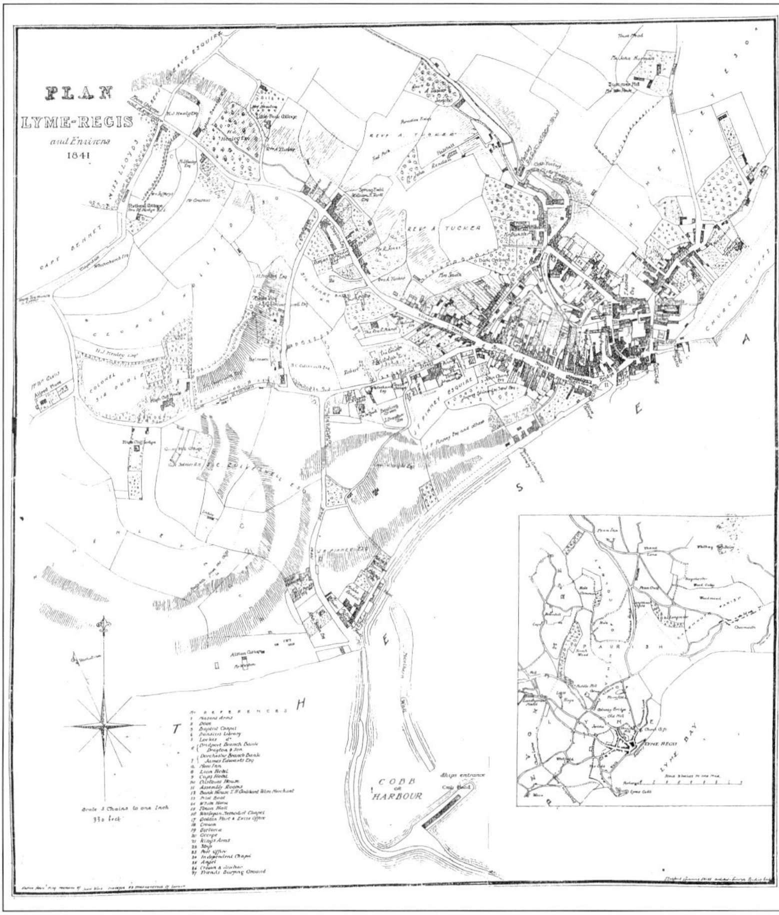

Plan of Lyme Regis 1841

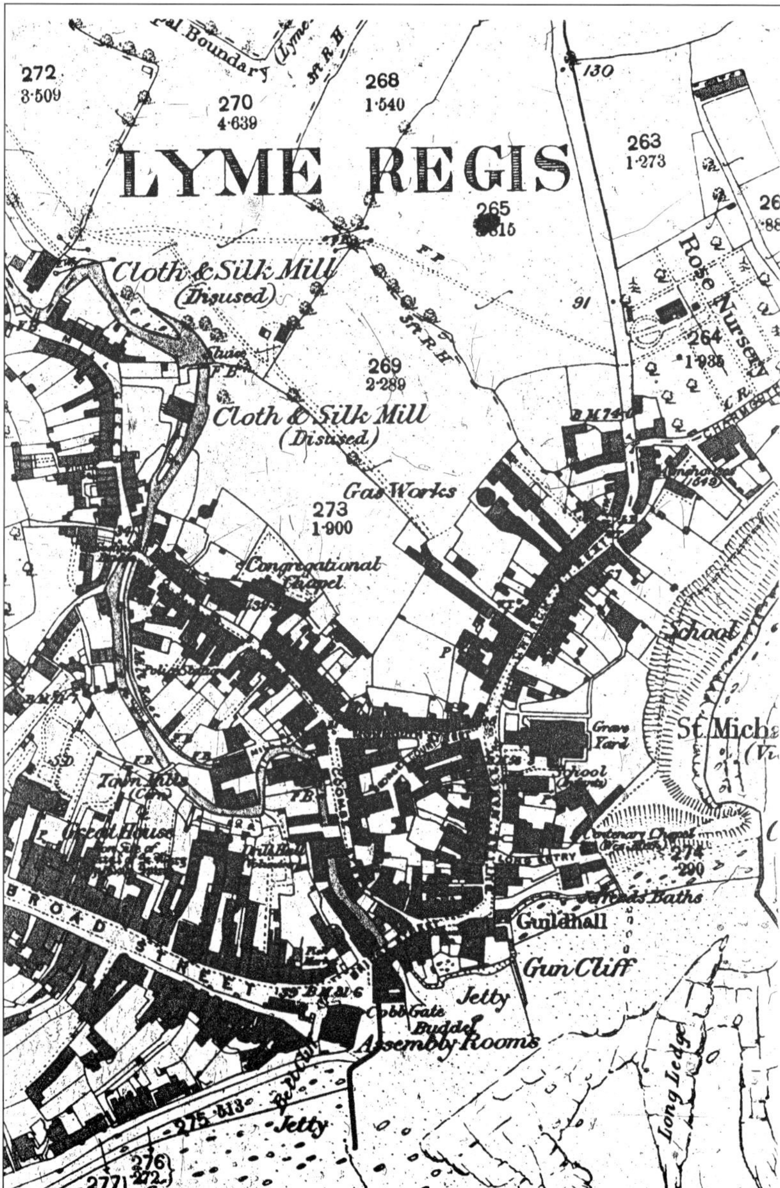

Ordnance Survey Map
1862 - 88

The earliest Tudor Map of Lyme Regis

Town Map 1825

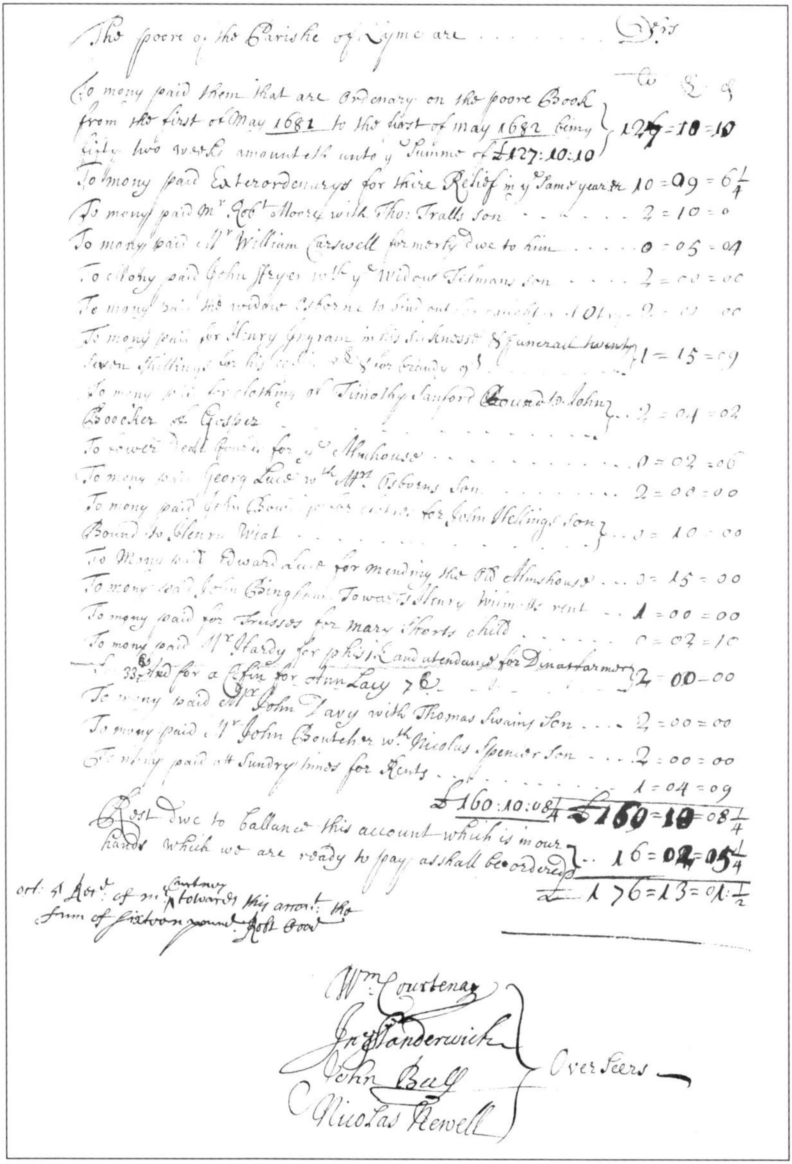

The poore of the Parishe of Lyme are .... Dr:rs

	£	s	d
To mony paid them that are Ordenary on the poore Booke from the first of May 1681 to the first of may 1682 being fifty two weeks amounteth unto ye Summe of £127:10:10	127	10	10
To mony paid Exterordenarys for there Relief in ye same year &c	10	09	6¼
To mony paid Mr. Robt Moore with Tho: Tralls son	2	10	0
To mony paid Mr William Carswell formerly dwe to him	0	05	04
To mony paid John Fryer with ye Widow Tilmans son	2	00	00
To mony paid the widow Osborne to bind out her daughter	2	00	00
To mony paid for Henry Gygram in his sicknesse & funerall twenty seven shillings for his coffin & for brandy	1	15	09
To mony paid for clothing of Timothy Sanford Bound to John Boocher of Gosper	2	04	02
To fower deal boards for ye Almhouse	0	02	06
To mony paid Georg Luce with Mrs Osborns son	2	00	00
To mony paid John Bound for his cloths for John Hellings son Bound to Henry Wiat	0	10	00
To Mony paid Edward Luce for mending the Old Almshouse	0	15	00
To mony paid John Bingham Towards Henry Wim... rent	1	00	00
To mony paid for trusses for mary Shorts child	0	02	10
To mony paid Mr Hardy for phisik and atendance for Dina Farmer £1 33s 6d for a coffin for Ann Lacy 7s 6d	2	00	00
To mony paid Mr John Lavy with Thomas Swains son	2	00	00
To mony paid Mr John Boutcher with Nicolus Spencer son	2	00	00
To mony paid att sundry times for Rents	1	04	09
£160:10:08¾	160	10	08¼
Rest dwe to ballance this account which is in our hands which we are ready to pay as shall be ordered	16	02	05¼
	176	13	01½

Rec'd of Mr Courtney towards this account the sum of sixteen pound Robt Good

Wm Courtenay
Jn Vanderwick
John Bull
Nicolas Newell
} Over Seers

From Poor Rate 1681

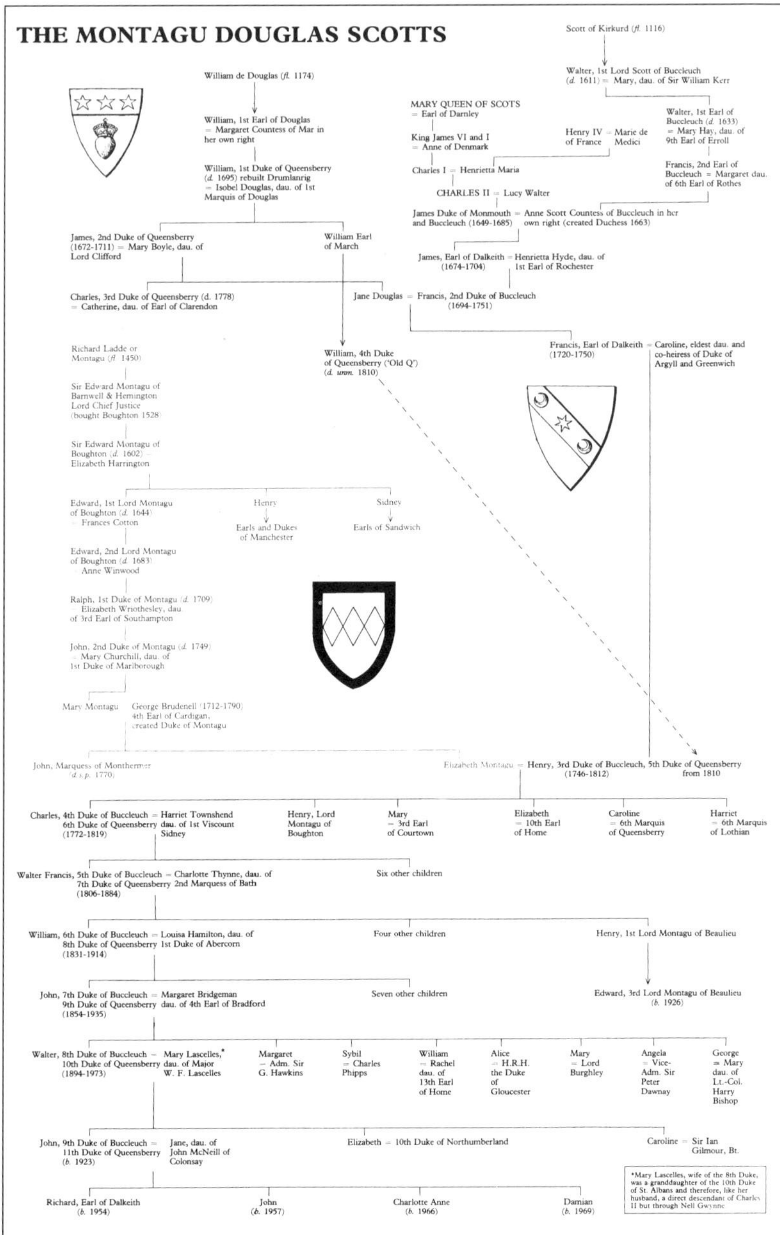

THE MONTAGU DOUGLAS SCOTTS
Scott of Kirkurd (fl. 1116)
Walter, 1st Lord Scott of Buccleuch (d. 1611) = Mary, dau. of Sir William Kerr
William de Douglas (fl. 1174)
MARY QUEEN OF SCOTS = Earl of Darnley
Walter, 1st Earl of Buccleuch (d. 1633) = Mary Hay, dau. of 9th Earl of Erroll
William, 1st Earl of Douglas = Margaret Countess of Mar in her own right
King James VI and I = Anne of Denmark
Henry IV = Marie de Medici of France
William, 1st Duke of Queensberry (d. 1695) rebuilt Drumlanrig = Isobel Douglas, dau. of 1st Marquis of Douglas
Charles I = Henrietta Maria
Francis, 2nd Earl of Buccleuch = Margaret dau. of 6th Earl of Rothes
CHARLES II = Lucy Walter
James Duke of Monmouth and Buccleuch (1649-1685) = Anne Scott Countess of Buccleuch in her own right (created Duchess 1663)
James, 2nd Duke of Queensberry (1672-1711) = Mary Boyle, dau. of Lord Clifford
William Earl of March
James, Earl of Dalkeith (1674-1704) = Henrietta Hyde, dau. of 1st Earl of Rochester
Charles, 3rd Duke of Queensberry (d. 1778) = Catherine, dau. of Earl of Clarendon
Jane Douglas = Francis, 2nd Duke of Buccleuch (1694-1751)
Richard Ladde or Montagu (fl. 1450)
William, 4th Duke of Queensberry ('Old Q') (d. unm. 1810)
Francis, Earl of Dalkeith (1720-1750) = Caroline, eldest dau. and co-heiress of Duke of Argyll and Greenwich
Sir Edward Montagu of Barnwell & Hemington Lord Chief Justice (bought Boughton 1528)
Sir Edward Montagu of Boughton (d. 1602) = Elizabeth Harrington
Edward, 1st Lord Montagu of Boughton (d. 1644) = Frances Cotton
Henry
Earls and Dukes of Manchester
Sidney
Earls of Sandwich
Edward, 2nd Lord Montagu of Boughton (d. 1683) = Anne Winwood
Ralph, 1st Duke of Montagu (d. 1709) = Elizabeth Wriothesley, dau. of 3rd Earl of Southampton
John, 2nd Duke of Montagu (d. 1749) = Mary Churchill, dau. of 1st Duke of Marlborough
Mary Montagu = George Brudenell (1712-1790) 4th Earl of Cardigan, created Duke of Montagu
John, Marquess of Monthermer (d.s.p. 1770)
Elizabeth Montagu = Henry, 3rd Duke of Buccleuch, 5th Duke of Queensberry from 1810 (1746-1812)
Charles, 4th Duke of Buccleuch 6th Duke of Queensberry (1772-1819) = Harriet Townshend dau. of 1st Viscount Sidney
Henry, Lord Montagu of Boughton
Mary = 3rd Earl of Courtown
Elizabeth = 10th Earl of Home
Caroline = 6th Marquis of Queensberry
Harriet = 6th Marquis of Lothian
Walter Francis, 5th Duke of Buccleuch 7th Duke of Queensberry (1806-1884) = Charlotte Thynne, dau. of 2nd Marquess of Bath
Six other children
William, 6th Duke of Buccleuch 8th Duke of Queensberry (1831-1914) = Louisa Hamilton, dau. of 1st Duke of Abercorn
Four other children
Henry, 1st Lord Montagu of Beaulieu
John, 7th Duke of Buccleuch 9th Duke of Queensberry (1854-1935) = Margaret Bridgeman dau. of 4th Earl of Bradford
Seven other children
Edward, 3rd Lord Montagu of Beaulieu (b. 1926)
Walter, 8th Duke of Buccleuch 10th Duke of Queensberry (1894-1973) = Mary Lascelles,* dau. of Major W. F. Lascelles
Margaret = Adm. Sir G. Hawkins
Sybil = Charles Phipps
William = Rachel dau. of 13th Earl of Home
Alice = H.R.H. the Duke of Gloucester
Mary = Lord Burghley
Angela = Vice-Adm. Sir Peter Dawnay
George = Mary dau. of Lt.-Col. Harry Bishop
John, 9th Duke of Buccleuch 11th Duke of Queensberry (b. 1923) = Jane, dau. of John McNeill of Colonsay
Elizabeth = 10th Duke of Northumberland
Caroline = Sir Ian Gilmour, Bt.
*Mary Lascelles, wife of the 8th Duke, was a granddaughter of the 10th Duke of St. Albans and therefore, like her husband, a direct descendant of Charles II but through Nell Gwynne
Richard, Earl of Dalkeith (b. 1954)
John (b. 1957)
Charlotte Anne (b. 1966)
Damian (b. 1969)

Family Tree

The Roman Villa showing the area of the bath house

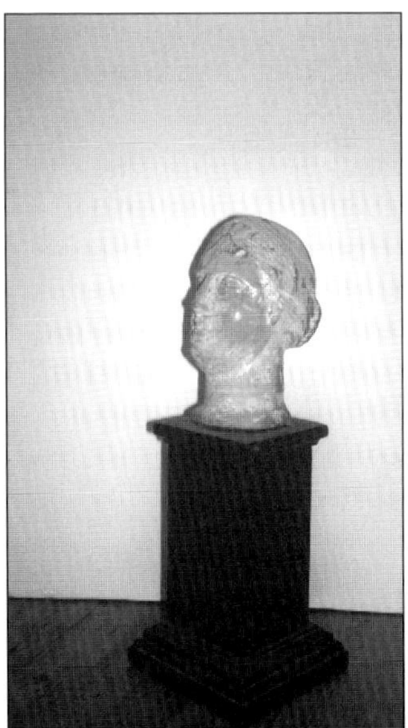

Roman head thought to have
been excavated locally

Thomas Coram by Wm Hogarth

The French Admiral de Tourville 1690

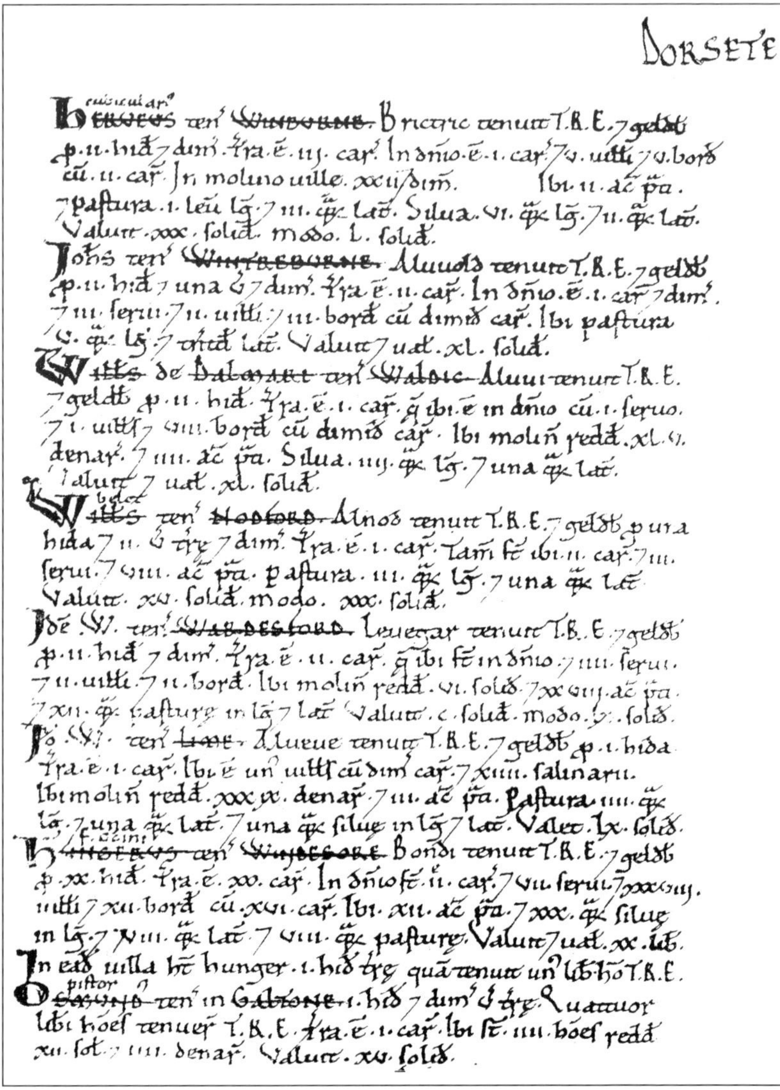

DORSETE.

H cubicular⁹ ~~erueus~~ ten' ~~Winborne~~. Brictric tenuit T.R.E. 7 geldb
p. ii. hid 7 dim. Tra. e. iii. car. In dnio. e. i. car. 7 v. uitti 7 v. bord
cu. ii. car. In molino uille. xxii d dim. Ibi. ii. ac pti.
7 pastura. i. leu lg. 7 iii. qx lat. Silua. vi. qx lg. 7 ii. qx lat.
Valuit. xxx. solid. modo. L. solid.
Iohs ten' ~~Wintreburne~~. Aluuold tenuit T.R.E. 7 geldb
p. ii. hid 7 una v 7 dim. Tra. e. ii. car. In dnio. e. i. car 7 dim.
7 iii. serui. 7 ii. uitti. 7 iii. bord cu dimid car. Ibi pastura
v. qx lg. 7 tntd lat. Valuit 7 uat. xl. solid.
W ~~itts~~ de ~~Dalmari~~ ten' ~~Walditc~~ Aluui tenuit T.R.E.
7 geldb p. ii. hid. Tra. e. i. car. q ibi. e in dnio cu. i. seruo.
7 i. uitts 7 viii. bord cu dimid car. Ibi molin redd. xl. v.
denar. 7 iiii. ac pti. Silua. iiii. qx lg. 7 una qx lat.
Valuit 7 uat. xl. solid.
W belet ~~itts~~ ten' ~~Wodford~~. Alnod tenuit T.R.E. 7 geldb p una
hida 7 ii. v tre 7 dim. Tra. e. i. car. Tam st ibi. ii. car. 7 iii.
serui. 7 viii. ac pti. Pastura. iii. qx lg. 7 una qx lat.
Valuit. xv. solid. modo. xxx. solid.
Ide W. ten' ~~Wardesford~~. Leuegar tenuit T.R.E. 7 geldb
p. ii. hid 7 dim. Tra. e. ii. car. q ibi st in dnio. 7 iiii. serui.
7 ii. uitti. 7 ii. bord. Ibi molin redd. vi. solid. 7 xxviii. ac pti.
7 xii. qx pasture in lg 7 lat. Valuit. c. solid. modo. [illegible]. solid.
Id W. ten' ~~Lime~~. Alueue tenuit T.R.E. 7 geldb p. i. hida.
Tra. e. i. car. Ibi e un uitts cu dim car. 7 xiiii. salinarii.
Ibi molin redd. xxxix. denar. 7 iii. ac pti. Pastura. iiii. qx
lg. 7 una qx lat. 7 una qx silue in lg 7 lat. Valet. lx. solid.
H f. [illegible] ~~[illegible]~~ ten' ~~[illegible]~~ Bondi tenuit T.R.E. 7 geldb
p. xx. hid. Tra. e. xx. car. In dnio st. ii. car. 7 vii. serui. 7 xxxiiii.
uitti 7 xii. bord cu. xvi. car. Ibi. xii. ac pti. 7 xxx. qx silue
in lg. 7 viii. qx lat. 7 viii. qx pasture. Valuit 7 uat. xx. lib.
In ead uilla ht hunger. i. hid tre qua tenuit un lib ho T.R.E.
O pistor ~~[illegible]~~ ten' in ~~Galtone~~. i. hid 7 dim' v tre. Quattuor
libi hoes tenuer T.R.E. Tra. e. i. car. Ibi st. iiii. hoes redd
xii. sol. 7 iiii. denar. Valuit. xv. solid.

Facsimile of page from Domesday Book

The Gin Shop on the Cobb, once the ammunition store and named after the hoist set up on the wall and used to lift the powder and shot

The Town Stocks, now in the Museum

The staircase in the Tudor House showing the newal post made from a ship's mast

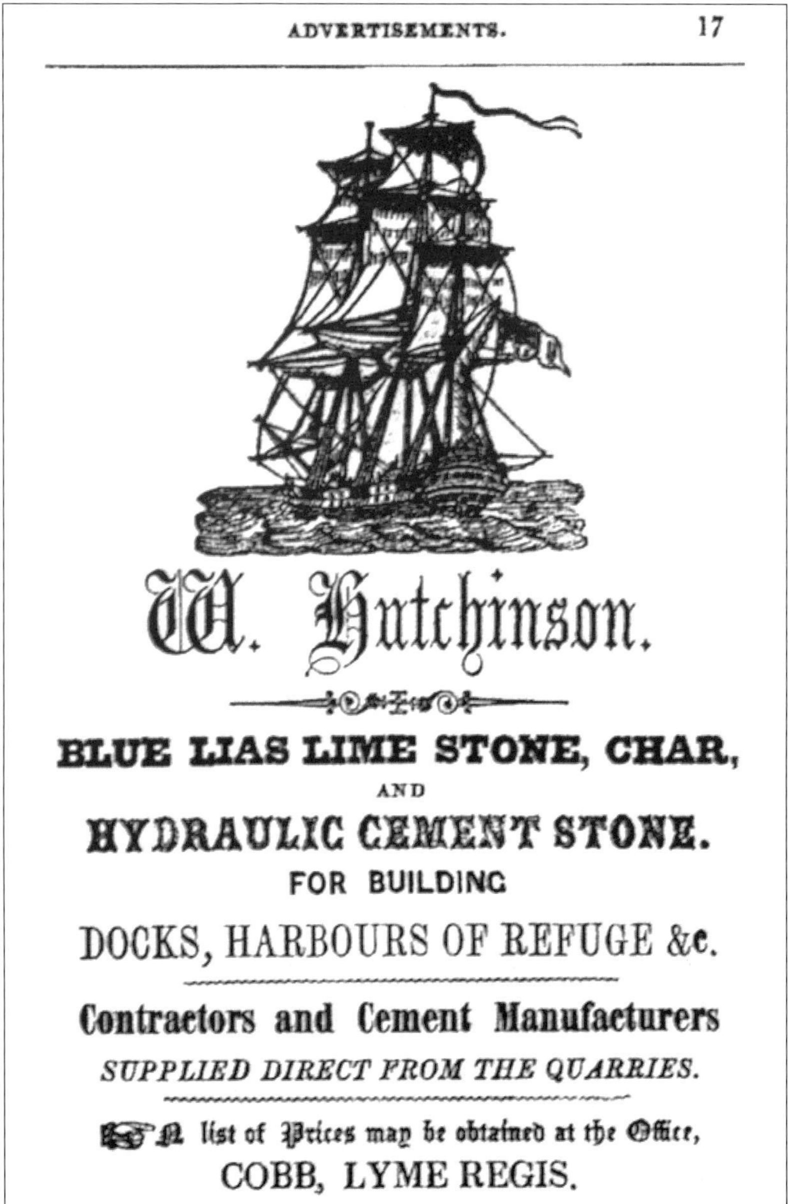

A Victorian advert for the Lyme stone industry near the Cobb

The Cement Works on Monmouth Beach, 1924

Broad Street before 1889

Company Sergeant Major Frederick Britton of the Royal Garrison Artillery, instructor of the Dorset Volunteer Artillery at Lyme Regis, 1897-1901. The Lyme company was nearly a hundred strong, and practised four times a week. The gun was for the repository drill, lifting the barrel out of its mounting with a gin-crane. There was fierce rivalry between the volunteer companies of the various Dorset towns, especially in the annual shooting competition

Mary Anning, 1799-1847
The famous Palaeontologist born in Lyme Regis

Gravestone in the cemetery of St Michael's Parish Church

William Pinney, MP for Lyme 1832 under the new Reform Act

~~To~~ The Earl of Shaftesbury Her Majesty's Lieutenant for the County of Dorset

MUSTER ROLL of the Persons enrolled and serving in the First Company of Dorset Artillery Volunteers commanded by Frederic Hinton.

EFFECTIVES ENTITLED TO EXEMPTION.

No.	Parish	Name	When Enrolled
1	Lyme Regis	Frederic Hinton	1 December 1859
2	"	George Cartwright	"
3	"	John George Sarsfield	
		Macnamara Moore	"
4	"	Robert Hillman	"
5	"	Robert William Hellman	"
6	"	Robert Radford, Junior	"
7	"	John Fowler	"
8	"	Charles Brown	"
9	"	Richard Fudge	"
10	"	Charles Snell	"
11	"	Henry Tucker	"
13	"	Walter Banfield Wallis	"
14	"	William Bennett	"
15	"	Mark Lawton	"
16	"	William Mansfield	"
18	"	Richard Dixon	"
19	"	Henry Radford	"
20	"	Henry Osborn	"
21	"	John Serrard	"
22	"	George Baker	"
23	"	John Harding	"
24	"	William Sturman	"
25	"	William French	"
26	"	Eli Dollin	"
27	"	Thomas Hoare	"
28	"	James Phillips Chick	"
29	"	George Govier	"
30	"	George Wood	"

Muster Roll

No.	Parish	Name	When Enrolled
31	Lyme Regis	John Channon	1 December 1859
32	"	Thomas Parrett	"
33	"	William Lucas	"
35	"	William Langford Junior	"
39	"	Jane Hingeston	"
40	Uplyme	John Godden	"
41	Lyme Regis	John Baker	"
42	"	George Boon	"
44	"	John Stevens	"
45	"	Charles Ball Junior	"
48	"	James Broom	"
49	"	George Hoare	"
50	"	Thomas Webber Jerrard	"
51	"	Walter Barns	"
52	"	George Symes	"
53	"	John Berry	"
57	Uplyme	John Edwards	"
58	Lyme Regis	William Whicker	3 January 1860
59	"	Philip Booth	"
60	"	George Gill	"
61	"	John Parsell	"
62	"	Thomas Edward Brown	12th "
64	"	James Stone	17th "
65	"	William John Jefferd	"
66	"	Frederick Cooke	"
67	Uplyme	Robert Judge	23rd "
68	Lyme Regis	Samuel Perkins	31st "
69	Uplyme	Henry Clapcott Jerrard	20 February "
70	Lyme Regis	George Barrett	22 " "
71	"	James Woodman	25 " "
73	"	George William Clarke	24 May "
74	"	Charles Steward	9 June "
75	"	Frederick Edwards	12 " "
76	"	Thomas Hitchcock	30 " "

Muster Roll

NON-EFFECTIVES.

No.	Parish	Name	When Enrolled
43	Lyme Regis	Henry Marder	1 December 1859
63	"	William Thorn	14 January 1860

Persons who have quitted the Corps

No.	Parish	Name	when enrolled
12	Lyme Regis.	Henry Franks Waring	1 December 1859
17	"	Robert Pidgeon	"
34	"	John Neal	"
36	"	William Gale	"
37	"	Charles Dyke	" } now Hon: Members
38	"	William James Atkins	" }
46	"	John Case	"
47	"	Samuel Pulsford	"
54	"	Arthur Boon	"
55	"	George Matthews	"
56	"	George Steward	"
72	Uplyme	William Randall	29 February 1860

Muster Roll

The Pilot Boat and the old fossil shop, 1890

Silver Street

Broad Street about 1900

The Fulling Tower on Coombe Street was built about 1830 to try a patent process for fulling cloth by steaming

A Lyme walking funeral
This one of John Groves, landlord of the Red Lion

CHAPTER FIVE
RELIGION

Mary Tudor, the Roman Catholic Queen, described Lyme as 'a heretic town.'[26] She meant the inhabitants did not subscribe to the Faith she believed in. One hundred years after her death, many of the townsfolk were to side with the Puritan Parliamentarians. Wanklyn, a local historian, wrote that the townsfolk were Puritan through and through, and there is no doubt that the messages from Geneva had more force than those from Rome or even Canterbury. It is an interesting speculation that the existence of the harbour might have helped Lyme to look outwards across the sea, not only in terms of trade but also in terms of receiving the harsh predestination ethic from extreme Protestantism in mainland Europe. It is certainly true that many foreign sailors coming into Lyme often chose to worship in the Baptist Church.[27] The Duke of Monmouth landed in Lyme not only because it was easy to do so on the shallow beach, but also because he had been told that many local Protestants would welcome and support him. Indeed Puritanism moved quickly from rejecting the time-honoured signs and ceremonies in religion, like for example wearing copes and surplices or having rings at marriage, to making serious attempts to introduce Nonconformist tokens into the Established Church. This strident activism in religious observance was intensified because there was also a considerable body of recusants who wanted to return to the pre-Reformation religious practices which had accommodated all the people and had not been divisive. Lyme experienced a good deal of Puritan fragmentation but it is significant that there were enough recusants in Lyme to justify the building of a Roman Catholic church in the nineteenth century.

It is difficult to find clear evidence about whether the religious attitude of many people was dissent or nonconformity, and the difference is important in the history of the town. Was it a place in which the Protestant ideas so vociferously proclaimed were the expression of deeply held spiritual beliefs, or were they rather the expression of a free and independent spirit? Was dissent, which was and still is a permanent force in the town, a disguise for political activity riding on the back of piety?

The roots of Christianity in Lyme are equally speculative, though it is known that the conversion of Dorset was completed in 705. Cynegils, the King of Wessex, had been baptised by Birinus, a missionary who became first Bishop of the West Saxons in 635. This was early for such missionary advance because St Augustine had only landed in Kent in 597. So Dorset was converted to Christianity within 38 years. Aldhelm was consecrated the first Bishop of Sherborne in 705. In 1075 the Diocese was transferred to Old Sarum, then to Salisbury, to Bristol in 1542, and much later, in 1836, was placed back in Salisbury.

The building of Lyme Parish Church, dedicated to St Michael the Archangel, was the earliest permanent building; it was begun in 1130 though not consecrated until 1298 as the result of a Visitation by Bishop Simon of Ghent who ordered there should be no delay. Traces of the earliest Norman building can still be seen in the west porch pillars but there have been many equally interesting additions to it in later times. They include the seventeenth-century oak lectern, the wall monuments, the canopied pulpit, and the nineteenth-century stained glass.

The building represents a significant part of the physical record of the history of the town.

Contrasting early records come from other quarters, including several Papal instructions. For example, Pope Eugenius III in 1145 confirmed the grant of Lyme and its fishing to the Abbey of Sherborne. Pope Clement VI, in 1383, granted Indulgences to those who contributed to the Leper Hospital, which gave them remission of temporal punishment due to sins; this Hospital was dedicated to the Blessed Virgin and the Holy Spirit, and was part of a residential settlement of small houses grouped round a square which extended to Broad Street. Slightly earlier than this, a group of mendicant or begging Carmelite friars, called the White Friars, had an oratory and a small house in Lyme. They had been formed during the Crusades and had come to England in 1246. It is not known where the oratory was situated but it is most likely to have been in Sherborne Lane where so many of the religious houses were built in every generation except the present; this is because it was one of the important routeways in and out of the town. Sea salt was taken to Sherborne Abbey along it, and travellers would come down it to get to the Cobb and sail away.

Until the Act of Toleration in 1689, which allowed Protestant Nonconformists to hold public religious meetings and establish their own chapels, worship would be conducted in the parish churches at Lyme and Uplyme. Lyme had several vicars who were eccentric. Rev Bartholomew Wesley, the great-grandfather of the eighteenth-century revivalist was 'intruded', or forced upon the parish, by Parliament, and several people in the church refused to accept his ministrations. For example, it was noted in the Dean of Salisbury's Visitation of 1635 that John Deane of Lyme Regis was presented for 'refusing to receive the communion of Mr Wes(t)ley.' A few years later, Rev Amos Short, Vicar from 1650 to 1662, was evicted under the Conventicle Act and established, illegally, an Independent Church. Two hundred years later, the long serving Rev F. P. Hodges, Vicar from 1833 to 1870, is noteworthy for starting the first schools, in what is now the parish rooms, and stopping the 'walking funeral' by insisting on the use of carriages; this made it difficult, and sometimes impossible, for most people to afford a funeral at all. He went about the town wearing jabot and silk stockings and was nicknamed the Bishop of Lyme, and he made it clear that 'he would not give an inch to dissenters.'

The Parish Church of St Peter and St Paul, in the adjacent parish of Uplyme, is in the Diocese of Exeter, and has had a contrasting history. In 774 King Cynewulf gave the Manor of Uplyme to the monastery of Glastonbury which was later confirmed by King Athelstan. This connection with Glastonbury continued until the Dissolution of the Monasteries, at which stage the advowson, or the right to present or nominate to a vacant living, was bought by the landowning Drake family of Musbury who kept it until 1775. During this long period, Uplyme became part of the routeway taken by the troops or supporters who were coming from or going to Lyme.

The building can be described as modernised medieval, and the largest remnant of the early church is the tower. This has contained bells since at least 1557 though they have been regularly re-cast and re-hung since then. The whole church was heavily restored in 1876, but the original structure can still be seen in the fourteenth-century arcade and the arch leading to the tower. The pulpit, comparable to the one in Lyme, was made in 1616 though its sounding board has been taken elsewhere.

The present Devon Hotel, situated on the main road, used to be the Uplyme Rectory until 1934. Long before it was a rectory it had been a monastery, and the catacombs in part of the cellar were probably the burial place for the monastery. It is believed that there used to be a secret tunnel from the catacombs to the church, but if it did exist it is now filled in.[28]

Several of the Rectors are worthy of note. Henry Morgan became Bishop of St David's in 1550 during the reign of Mary Tudor. John Godwin was intruded during the Commonwealth in 1650 and deprived in 1663. Nicholas Vere was Rector from 1769 to 1809, and was a Prebendary of Wells and Winchester Cathedrals at the same time.

Dissent in Lyme has always been strong and is expressed in several contrasting ways which are often political. In religion Dissent is sometimes associated with mainland European ideas like those coming from the Anabaptists, or Calvin and Zwingli in Switzerland, or Luther in Germany. We know that visiting sailors often worshipped with the Baptists when they docked in Lyme, and it is not too far-fetched to assume that the schismatic religious ideas came by sea as well. We have already commented many times that the sea is the most powerful influence on the town and it is important that this influence of communication by sea should not be excluded from religious considerations; it probably explains, in part, why there have been so many different sects in the town.

As soon as one sect started a chapel or created a regular meeting this would be the sign for another to be created. In the days when it was illegal to hold public meetings, preachers and their followers would hold secret prayer meetings at Whitechapel Rock in the Undercliff, or in Sleech Wood. The earliest formal group of Puritans was the Baptists. They were bound up with the Western Baptist Association and therefore were associated from the start with the earlier Baptist Chapel in Kilmington.[29] Their first record is of 'An Assembly of Protestant Dissenters who scrupled the baptising of infants.' It is contained in their precious Minute Book which was started in 1653, their foundation year, which coincidentally was the year in which Cromwell became Lord Protector and John Bunyan was baptised at the age of 25. The Lyme Baptists held their immersion or dipping in the river at the bottom of Woodmead Road, which is why, in that area, there are roads named Jordan, Jericho, Paradise and Bethel. Baptists were very prominent in the Siege of Lyme, and in the Monmouth Rebellion, and many were subsequently punished for their participation by hanging, quartering or victimisation. Mayor Alford, a Royalist Major, led an attack against the local Puritans and especially against the Baptists which included the hanging of their Minister, Rev Sampson Locke.

The Society of Friends, the Quakers, were a different religious group with considerable support, but who by contrast with the Baptists did not suffer serious persecution. Their Meeting House in Coombe Street was taken down 100 years ago, and their burial ground was a walled enclosure at the entrance to Stile Lane, now covered by a modern bungalow.[30] It has been suggested that they were too prosperous to arouse serious opposition either in the town or from the clergy. It is rarely wise to persecute those who give money or employment and the Friends gave both. A comparable but essentially different group were the Plymouth Brethren who met in another house which was also in Coombe Street.

The Methodists were never very popular in the town. They met first at 334 Sherborne Lane, but this meeting-place was replaced in 1839 by a custom-built chapel in Church Street. But it was always a minority who supported the Methodists, possibly because the other Nonconformists had been around for so much longer and could depend upon more traditional support. They never made much headway and the chapel was eventually pulled down to be replaced by some flats in 1978.

Roman Catholicism never died in Lyme but was often practised in secret. In general however, recusancy flourished outside the town rather than in it. The Catholic Church, situated on Silver Street, is dedicated to Saints Michael and George. It was built between 1835 and 1837, and the Lady Chapel in 1851. The interesting fact is that the church was needed at all in such an anti-papist town. It suggests that there were more Roman Catholic families living in Lyme than most people would have guessed.

Religious Postscript: The Lyme Regis Tapestry

This tapestry shows men and women in some ceremony which could be a wedding or a coronation. It is large, measuring 17 feet by 11 feet 6 inches, and has recently been restored by a local group of needlewomen with guidance from experts at Hampton Court Palace. It has been hanging in Lyme Regis Parish Church again since 1996 after an absence of 20 years, having been on loan to the National Trust. It was originally purchased by Rev Edward Peak in 1886 who gave it to the church.

The subject of the tapestry is of considerable interest. It has been suggested that it shows the marriage of Henry VII to Elizabeth of York. This would make the blonde hair of the principal lady in the picture eminently appropriate because Elizabeth had blonde hair. However it has been guessed that it was woven in Brussels in 1495 which does not tie in quite so neatly with other known relevant dates. Henry VII married Elizabeth in 1486 and was crowned in 1487. Perhaps such fine tuning of dates is not possible.

The rival claims for commemoration on the panel all involve Catherine of Aragon, either as one of the crowd, or on the occasion of her first marriage to Prince Arthur or her second marriage to Henry VIII. It is known that Catherine was an expert needlewoman, which does not necessarily imply that she would depict herself but rather that she could well have been involved in the sewing of the tapestry. Whoever is represented on the panel was clearly important and the whole Renaissance work is of outstanding quality.

CHAPTER SIX

POVERTY AND HEALTH

In an unpublished paper on nineteenth-century censuses, quoted earlier, Dennis Mills writes: 'Grinding poverty was undoubtedly the lot of people in nineteenth-century Dorset.' Joan Walker wrote in 1981 that there was 'gross poverty and overcrowding'[31] in Victorian Lyme and there is no doubt that the living conditions of the people in earlier times would have been no better. This is mainly because the medieval town plan, which can still be detected quite easily, had kept to the original 45 acres around Coombe Street and alongside the river. The land to east and west was unstable, and the Colway Tithings prevented expansion in that direction. There was thus a long standing acceptance of congestion and squalor. Whole families lived in one room, and several families would have shared the same water supply and the same lavatories with the river serving both functions.

Leprosy was fairly common in medieval Europe. A loathsome disease which slowly eats away the body and forms shiny white scales on the skin, in early times it was often used to describe any serious infection of the skin. There was a square of leper houses in Lyme arranged around an enclosure, built in 1336, and dedicated to the 'Blessed Virgin and the Holy Spirit.' The well is still there. In 1383 the Pope granted indulgences to those who contributed alms for the repair of the bell-tower.

Another scourge, the Black Death, arrived in England in 1349 and fanned out from the ports. As Lyme was an important port at this time it is likely that some of the black rats which carried the rat flea arrived here, despite there being no evidence to support this theory nor records of any townsfolk getting the dreaded disease.

The health of the town was closely linked with the introduction of the Elizabethan Poor Law in 1601 which established the responsibility of each township for its poor. This law had been passed at a time of national unrest caused by the introduction of field enclosures which had taken away 'the very commons, whereupon many townships do live.' As a result there was unemployment, hunger, and often distressing poverty. There is evidence that such hardship existed in Lyme but it was relieved in part by the availability of local fish. The Annual Reports of the Overseers of the Poor, appointed by the local magistrates and reporting to the Vestry, record those who received relief. Most help was given to widows, some to children, especially orphans, and some for the repair of almshouses. The money distributed during any year was never more than £100 throughout the seventeenth century.

The deeper implication of the Poor Law was that every workman was regarded as a potential pauper and slowly became wholly or partly dependent upon relief. It is difficult to over-exaggerate the effect of this social, economic dependence because it was almost impossible to escape the condition of pauperism. It was intensified by the Act of Settlement of 1662 which decreed that poor persons could settle in another township only if they obtained a Certificate of Settlement. This made the population much less mobile and the effect of the enforced immobility lasted until 1795 when only those who did not receive relief were exempt. The Speenhamland Decision (1795) for outdoor relief (that which could be obtained without being residential) based help on the price of bread and the size of the family. This encouraged farmers to pay their labourers less because they knew the wages would be made up by the Poor Law.

The Elizabethan system of poor relief remained in force, with a few modifications, until the Whig Poor Law Reform Act of 1834. The essential change that came with the 1834 Act was the complete replacement of outdoor relief by relief in workhouses set up and managed by the Poor Law Unions. Lyme belonged to the Axminster Union as part of the group of 17 parishes which also included Uplyme. From a Poor Law view the county boundary between Dorset and Devon did not exist. The Axminster workhouse was built in 1836, two years after the Act had been passed, and cost £7,000; it was extended four years later at a cost of £2,500 and had room for 450 paupers. It replaced an earlier building built in 1613 which had been partly financed from the tolls of the Bridport Turnpike.

The Axminster Guardians Minute Book, 1836-38, lists the area served which includes Lyme with Axmouth, Beer and Seaton, Colyton, Coombepyne, Musbury, Shute, Uplyme and Charmouth. The Guardians included Sir John Talbot, A.H.D. Acland, Rev Hodges and Rev Ethelstone. The regular entries tell of the struggles of the poor and involve such small amounts of money, but one or two deserve special mention because of their local interest. One records that Joseph Love of the Parish of Lyme Regis applied for a loan of 10 shillings to assist him in his present necessities. Another dated 1 June 1837 from Messrs Wildey and Co., 3 Agar Street, Strand asking for funds 'to supply the Union with Cocoa Nut Fibre for Bedding' later stipulates that 'bread was to be made of best wheaten flour instead of the best seconds as hitherto.' On 20 April 1837, the Overseers of Lyme Regis 'be allowed to expend the sum of 20 shillings in procuring stones and lodging them in some convenient place for the purpose of setting Paupers of that Parish out of employ to work in cracking them.'

E.C. Tufnell's Report on the State of the Labourers in Dorset, c.1844, comments 'in a great part of this district wages are so low, that they cannot fall, and the distress of the country does not affect the labouring classes. Their normal state is one of the deepest deprivations to lower which should be to depopulate the land.' The diet for an able-bodied man in the Cerne Abbas Union in 1838, which would not be very different from the diet at Axminster, was as follows: 6 oz bread and 1½ pints of gruel for breakfast, 4 oz cooked meat, 1½ pints of soup and 6 oz potatoes for dinner, 6 oz bread with 1½ pints of soup for supper.

By contrast Jo Draper, quoting F. J. H. Darton, writes of a different meal enjoyed in the Red Lion in Lyme in 1890, when for 2s 6d was eaten 'dressed crab (lots and lots of it), Easter lamb, real Dorset lamb, Blue Vinney in good condition and in its proper state – a whole cheese.' Earlier, during the eighteenth century, the quality of the food prepared and served for those visiting Lyme as a seaside alternative to Bath was high, and along with it, by association, would have been a commensurate improvement in the food available for those who prepared it; one rarely sees a thin cook.

The most subtle change in everyday diet, and consequently of the health of the town, was caused by the arrival of grocery shops in working class districts during the eighteenth century. Though these were simple and basic by modern standards, the possibility of buying food rather than having to live on what one could catch or grow for oneself revolutionised life. Food for basic living slowly became easily accessible and at the same time there also came a major revolution in domestic economics. There was less living by barter and an increasing need to pay for food. Survival and wellbeing thus depended increasingly upon having a wage.

Lyme was a major port until the merchant ships got too big, so that not all the visiting sailors attended the Baptist Chapel but preferred the cosy company of individual women. Some women who were willing to give such pleasure are reputed to have put their brooms outside their front doors when their husbands were away. What is not clear is how the lonely sailors knew the sign so perhaps it was really designed for local residents. There can be little doubt that prostitution existed and little doubt also that it brought in its train the usual venereal diseases. Good health not only depended upon having enough food but sometimes upon appropriate medication as well.

Joan Walker's paper on child mortality and public health covers the period 1856 to 1979. She writes of 72 burials in 1857 of infants and young adults of which 39 were of children under 16 years of age, which is 57%, and at all other times in the same century the percentage of deaths of children was very high. Some died in epidemics of smallpox, scarlet fever, and measles. Others suffered and were debilitated through working too hard in the local silk and lace factories. In 1861, 25 children between 8 and 15 were employed in the silk mill, but by 1871 legislation prevented the employment of children under 11.

The first Medical Officer of Health was Richard Bangay, a local GP who took office in 1882 and first reported in 1886. He was critical of the bad housing and sanitation in the town and made special mention of slaughterhouses, bakeries, dairies and artisan dwellings. He also commented on the water supply and complained that the foul openings of the drains emptying into the river were too high, and by 1895 this had been corrected. The next Medical

Officer, James Spurr, was able to complete the installation of the new water supply which was officially turned on by the Mayor at Horn Bridge in 1896. It replaced the independent wells and springs which could no longer supply the increased amount of water needed in general terms but especially for the new flushing water closets.

The first cottage hospital was in Providence Place in Sherborne Lane and was used between 1873 and 1889. After a short stay in Keble Cottage above Holmbush fields, the hospital moved to the Gables opposite the Church where it operated effectively for 30 years. There was built, at the personal expense of Arthur Lister, the brother of the famous medical scientist, the first antiseptic and aseptic operating theatre in Lyme. In 1927 the hospital finally moved to Hernlee on Pound Road where it served the community for 67 years. It eventually became a private nursing home in 1994. Medical arrangements for the town in that year were taken over by a group of general practitioners and ancillary staff, in a custom built medical centre on Uplyme Road. In addition to the hospital provision, two rooms at the end of the Cobb were used for many years in the nineteenth century as a small isolation hospital. When foreign ships were suspected of carrying sailors with infectious diseases, the isolation rooms enabled the suspects to be put into quarantine until the medical doubts were resolved. The building was also used for some severe cases of tuberculosis. It is now the Sailing Club.

The range and incidence of specific epidemics analysed by Joan Walker provides a valuable commentary on the general state of health in the town. With the exception of cholera which did not reach Lyme, the town seems to have fallen prey to all the major scourges which swept through the country, and local doctors claimed that the epidemics were brought by land and not by sea. Smallpox was a frequent scourge until the 1853 Act required children to be vaccinated before the age of three months. There was an outbreak of scarlet fever in 1856 which continued until 1859 and resulted in the deaths of many children under five. Diphtheria was more difficult to diagnose during the nineteenth century but it must have existed in the town. Measles was easier to identify and caused the deaths of many children; for example, it accounted for four deaths in 1857 and 18 in 1869. In 1888 Dr Bangay reported that two thirds of the town's children suffered from the disease and in 1902 Dr Spurr closed three schools for a fortnight. Whooping cough continued to recur and caused many deaths, a sad fact which prevailed over the whole country until there was adequate vaccination in the 1940s. Typhoid broke out in 1889 and caused serious illness and death; it was thought to have been caused by the drain from Church Street, and the slaughterhouse flow, fouling the river at the bottom of Coombe Street. An investigation by Dr Spurr reported: 'The drains and closets of the surrounding cottages were inspected and found very defective and notices being served upon the owner' who was the major landowner, Colonel Henley. Tuberculosis killed two or three victims each year during the nineteenth century and was eventually eradicated, but it did not become a notifiable disease until 1912.

Many, if not all, of these health problems were exacerbated by the unsatisfactory state of the sewers which were only repaired or improved in piecemeal fashion until 1995 when the whole system was replaced. This latest major development included a re-sculpturing of the Gunnery Walk and the area in front of the Museum and the Marine Theatre.

Lyme has produced several noteworthy men in the field of medicine and hygiene. One was Dr John Case (1680-

1700), an astrologer in the reign of James II, who lived in Lambeth and wrote and practised astrology, anatomy and medicine. Another was Thomas Coram (1688-1751), who opened the Foundling Hospital in London and was later made a Freeman of the town. Most distinguished was Joseph Lister (1827-1912), who adopted Lyme as his town though he was born in London; his work in the field of antiseptic surgery revolutionised medicine. He was knighted, made a baron, awarded the Order of Merit and was President of the Royal Society, 1894-1900. He lived at High Cliff which is now divided into flats.

It may be of interest to include a comment about the work of the barber-surgeons whose names are known but not the precise work they did. For centuries they were the only form of medical help; they would cut hair, extract a tooth, use leeches, and in emergencies they would be asked to perform various complicated surgical operations. How sad that we only know their names and not any precise local information about their role and the stories they could tell about the health of the people.

CHAPTER SEVEN

EDUCATION

The first formal education was centred on the church but there is no record of the earliest school groups. What existed in those medieval days would be only for the education of boys. Girls learned what they had to learn in the kitchen with their mothers. Most boys at a very young age would learn how to work and live alongside men in local trades such as fishing, boat building, weaving, milling, building and farming. They would learn about the responsibilities of being in the family. They would also learn, while they were still young, how to live with little money, how to make friends, how to live with neighbours, and how to be an accepted part of their own local community. This informal education was the bedrock not only of the learning process in Lyme but of the whole country until industry revolutionised the process. It did not, however, revolutionise Lyme, which did not choose to copy the north in the textile trades nor in any other. For example, when Lyme had too shallow a draught for the more popular but larger boats, the town gave up shipbuilding.

One of the earliest schools of which there is a record was started by the local historian George Roberts. It was based in Monmouth House at the top of Broad Street and offered an education in Classics and Mathematics. It opened in 1844 and closed in 1856. Canon Liddon was one of the more distinguished pupils. There were probably

appreciation that one realised how "out of the mouths of babes and sucklings Thou has perfected praise".' Thirteen air-raid warnings were sounded during school hours during the 1939-45 war.

The numbers of infants increased after the war and it was necessary and possible to move out of the old building and into the new which opened on King's Way in September 1975. This released room in the old building but soon even this became cramped as well as unsuitable for modern methods and techniques and so the juniors moved to the same site as the infants. At last all the children from 5 to 11 were under the same roof in modern buildings.

Secondary

It was in 1923 that A. J. Woodroffe, the Chairman of Dorset Education Committee, decided there should be a Secondary School in Lyme Regis separate from the Senior part of the Church School. He was also vice-chairman of the County Council and Chairman of the Finance Committee, so his opinion carried a considerable amount of weight. This man of power chose the Woodmead Halls as the site of his project. They were a set of huts on the site of what is now the Leisure Centre. The Board of Education, as it was then, claimed there were not enough pupils to justify a grammar school in the area but Woodroffe was keen to have one. He visited every house in the town where there was a child who was eligible to take the entrance exam, often arriving in his chauffeur-driven car. He then personally invigilated the exam behind locked doors. Every child passed which created a national record for any selection exam. His only regret was that he had always planned that the grammar school should be a boys only school but in the end he needed the girls to swell the numbers and so it was a co-educational school from the start.

The first head was Mr Greenshields who stayed for four years and then went on to run Poole Grammar School. Meanwhile County Councillor Woodroffe had not stopped thinking about the new grammar school and decided that the Woodmead huts would have to be replaced. He asked the County architect to design a new school but when he saw the plans he tore them up because he wanted a more public school style of building. Eventually the design was approved and the school cost £19,000 to build. The builder went bankrupt because he had used wet sand from the beach in his cement and much of it had to be replaced at great expense.

Throughout this period, W. H. Thomas was second master and continued in that office for several years; he was the distant ear of Woodroffe. S. L. Watton followed Greenshields as head and carried on efficiently during the war with the small school of 180 children. During one tragic week, his daughter contracted polio, his wife died, one son was killed and the other captured at Arnhem. Watton never recovered.

Fresh from military service, Thornton Pearn came in September 1946. He was 32, and the next youngest member of staff was about 50. He still had Thomas as second master. There was no sixth form unless you count one boy who was waiting to go to university and one girl who had to leave. During his first year Pearn believed his top priority was to establish a sixth form and by the end of the year he had been successful in recruiting 25 students. It also gave him the immediate reputation that he was ready to work hard and get to know the families who were patronising the school, and it was a public relations winner. He also wanted to start a parent-teacher association but the staff did not like the idea so he launched a parents association instead with no staff participation, because he thought it important that the links with parents should be strong.

Lyme was, however, still a small school of about 180 pupils and Pearn realised that he would soon have to compete with larger comprehensives at Bridport and Beaminster. He believed the only way to survive was to become comprehensive and he became even more convinced that action was required when plans were being discussed for the building of a secondary modern school next to the golf course, which would have replaced the senior part of the church school. There was also a wave of ideological and financial support for schools opting for comprehensive education but there was no money available for small grammar schools. County Councillor Woodroffe was still alive, though in his eighties, but his opposition was neutralised by the naming of the new school after him, and his being appointed the permanent vice-chairman of governors.

However, there were more girls than boys in the school and Pearn wanted a nearer equal balance. He opened a boys boarding house at St Andrew's in 1950 which took 30 boys at first and this was soon increased to 38. This then gave him a majority of boys, so a girls boarding house was created at Harcombe House in 1954/5 which took 60 boarding girls. To achieve a more permanent balance of the sexes, Harcombe House was eventually used for boys between 11 and 15 and senior boys were housed in St Andrew's. This was only possible when Rhode Hill House had been acquired and was able to take 80 girls. By 1970, there were 188 boarders, and this high number was sustained with a steady flow of applicants from abroad who all had to have British passports to comply with the rules about state education in this country.

Woodroffe School was thus largely conceived by two men who were not natives of the town but who loved and adopted it. Woodroffe was the founder who contrived the creation of a grammar school, and Pearn later rode on the tide of the popular socialist comprehensive ideology to keep the school alive. Having done so he broadened its base through boarding which balanced the gender differentiation, raised the academic standard and provided a context for local children to glimpse a world outside the town through their school friends. It is an unusual story when set against raging current philosophies about selective education, the advantages of a state boarding education, and the fashion of relying heavily upon outside consultants. The only consultants that mattered to the school in all these national disputations were two men, Woodroffe and Pearn.

Independent education was comparably distinctive. There was a Roman Catholic school adjacent to the Roman Catholic Church run by nuns of the Servants of the Sacred Heart who came in 1890 and moved to Bow House in Lyme in 1897. In 1903 their place was taken by the small Community of the Holy Child, but with their departure the school was closed despite the efforts of Mrs Talbot at Rhode Hill who had plans for expanding the school, which did not materialise.

After the 1939-45 war, the Sisters of St Gilda's, who belonged to a French Order called officially by the French Government the Sisters of Christian Instruction, and who had already had a convent school in Yeovil, set up a small school in Stile House on the Sidmouth Road which eventually closed and was sold up in 1966/7.

There was also a small private school in Uplyme run by Mrs North who eventually joined with a preparatory school at Hunter's Lodge.

Allhallows School, now College, at Rousdon, was the nearest public school but was always small in numbers though large in playing fields. It catered only for boys at the start though it is co-educational now. It had originally been based in Honiton and took over the Peek Mansion with its very spacious accommodation in 1938. It had a staircase made of Sicilian marble which had been gathered from a shipwreck on the beach; the mosaic floors were cut by convicts and sent to the mansion on trays. The stained glass windows include a fine one of the Duke of Monmouth. The number of boys attending from Lyme, however, was never very large.

The independent school which achieved an international reputation was Summerhill, started at Pine Crest, a three storey building with a grand portico entrance on the hill going out of Lyme towards Bridport. In 1924 A. S. Neill (1883-1973), a Scot fresh from teaching in Germany, chose Lyme to launch his educational experiment.[33] He wished to reduce fear in children and believed they should work through their fantasies, act out their aggression and talk about their fears. He accepted thieves, liars, bed-wetters, children with temper tantrums and a whole range of problem children. Children who were neglected, abandoned, troublesome, lazy, anti-social were given places. He accepted pupils who had been thrown out of public schools; Eton and Harrow supplied one boy each year. Ethel Mannin (1900-1984) visited Summerhill in 1925 and wrote: 'It was all very casual – a simple, comfortable, friendly sort of casualness, infinitely refreshing. The gates were painted black and orange.'

There was little understanding locally about what was going on at the school. Dorothy Bailey who cooked and mended there said that many of the townspeople thought they were a little mad. Neill himself wrote disparagingly of Lyme and regarded it as a class-conscious little town –

'we were outsiders.' The pupils had to go into the town in pairs, they swam on Monmouth Beach, went for runs and walks, and used a riding school at Uplyme. Outside Lyme, Neill was in great demand as a speaker and was eventually given an honorary degree at Exeter University, where it was necessary for him to wear a dinner suit for the occasion; he borrowed various parts of it from friends including the Professor of Education, Robin Pedley, who lived on the corner house in Coram Avenue and who had proposed him for the degree. The school had been founded in 1924 and moved to Leiston in Suffolk in 1932.

Nearby at Monkton Wyld was another experimental school founded by Carl and Eleanor Urban who provided boarding places for children separated from their families. It was non-competitive and run on the basis of a weekly policy meeting of staff and pupils.

Tertiary

When Nonconformist tutors were ejected from Oxford and Cambridge during the eighteenth century because they were unable to subscribe to the Test Acts, they went into the provinces to establish academies of their own. They were usually very successful and such centres were set up in several towns including Bristol, Exeter, Tiverton and Lyme Regis. The Lyme Academy was based upon the Baptist Church which had been the centre of Nonconformity for many years since before the Monmouth Rebellion.

The other evidence of tertiary education in the town came with the Lyme Regis and Charmouth Mechanics Institute which had its first annual meeting on 14 January 1845 at the end of its first year of existence. Sixteen lectures had been given by volunteer lecturers who included the local historian Roberts; only one lecturer was hired. The subjects covered self-culture, astronomy, physical geography, antiquities of Lyme Regis, the history of Egypt, natural history, botany, light, colour and vision, and chemistry. The total expenditure for the first year was £51.16.9½ and receipts were £60.7.0. The library had 250 volumes and there were 304 subscribing members. "All went well, and our politicians found out a secret worth knowing, that a liberal communication of our intellectual stores is the highest order of benefit we can confer on each other."[34] The President was the Mayor, and two Vice-Presidents were Major-General Sir D. Hill and Mr R. Hillman. Mr H. B. Farnall was the Chairman.

The movement to set up Mechanics Institutes had been begun by Dr George Birkbeck in London and the idea was soon supported by working-class leaders. In 1841 W. D. Gillon proposed that grants should be given to them, and although this was not approved by Parliament the movement grew quickly, especially in the industrial north. It is particularly interesting that the idea took root in Lyme because elsewhere it was largely patronised by the middle classes. In some towns, like Nottingham, the Institutes became centres for the university extension movement, and led to the foundation of some civic universities.

Scott Lowe

CHAPTER EIGHT

WRITERS, ARTISTS AND DESIGNERS

who have some connection with Lyme

Writers

Daniel Defoe (c. 1661-1731) stayed in Lyme in 1724. He had been a Dissenter who took part in Monmouth's rebellion and in 1688, at the age of 27, returned to Lyme and joined the forces of William III.

Henry Fielding (1707-1754) tried to abduct Sarah Andrew, the daughter of Andrew Tucker who lived in the Tudor House in Church Street. Her father and brother tried to catch him, so Fielding hurriedly departed and pinned a note to a post in the Square which said, 'This is to give notice to all the world that Andrew Tucker and his son John Tucker are clowns and cowards.'

William Wordsworth (1770-1850) stayed with a friend at Musbury which is between Axminster and Axmouth. Birdsmoorgate has been considered as a possible alternative inspiration for his poem on daffodils, to the more usual lakeland context. In 1796 he settled for a time, with his only sister, at Racedown.

Jane Austen (1775-1817) visited Lyme twice, in 1803 and 1804, when she lodged in Pyne House on Broad Street. She stayed for approximately three months on each occasion. She wrote *Persuasion* in Lyme in 1815 and it was published posthumously in 1818. In this novel, she describes the town: 'Its old wonders and new improvements, with the very beautiful line of cliffs stretching out to the east of the town, are what the stranger's eye will seek; and a very strange stranger it must be, who does not see charms in the immediate environment of Lyme, to make him wish to know it better.'[35] In a letter to her sister Cassandra sent from Lyme on Friday, 14 September 1804 she writes, 'I continue quite well in proof of which I have bathed again this morning. It was absolutely necessary that I should have the little fever and indisposition which I had; it has been all the fashion this week in Lyme. We are quite settled in our lodgings... tho' nothing can exceed the inconvenience of the offices, except the general dirtiness of the house and furniture, and all its inhabitants.'[36] Elsewhere the diary records that Mrs Austen played at 'commerce' (a card game) and Jane danced. They used parasols and beach bonnets but the hot weather 'kept us in a perpetual state of inelegance.' She also witnessed a fire which was caused by bringing furs from the attic while carrying a candle at Crossman's the baker. The fire destroyed 42 houses and the effect was so serious that it was necessary to serve meals at the Parish Church to feed the destitute.

Mary Russell Mitford (1787-1855) the novelist and dramatist stayed at the Great House.

Frederick Marryat (1792-1848) visited Lyme in 1819 which was also the year he became a Fellow of the Royal Society. He wrote many sea faring and other novels, including *Mr Midshipman Easy* and *Peter Simple*. He was in the Royal Navy for a spell and travelled extensively. He lived in Brussels, Canada and the USA. In 1843 he settled on his farm in Norfolk.

Francis Turner Palgrave (1824-1897) lived at Little Park in Lyme and his cousin married a Lister. He was great friends with Alfred, Lord Tennyson (1809-1892) and they went on great walks together in the Lyme area in 1867. As well as compiling the *Golden Treasury*, an anthology of poetry, he also published several books of poems which mentioned Lyme.

One in particular is worth quoting in full:-

Old Time his old hour turning,
Shall shake up the sand sublime,
Give Obstruction a jolly good churning
And hearts with alertness prime
And the Cobb (aye the Cobb they call'd it,
Since first it kept back the sea,
Yea, since the first trawler trawl'd it,)
Shall a Harbour of Refuge be.

Sailors, its topmasts running,
With shouts the shore shall shake;
Till the fossil of old Miss Anning
And her ammonites all awake.
And with one heart and one mouth,
We'll own the prophetic ditty
For truth, sung of old by Monmouth,
That Lyme should be yet a City.

published by E. Locke, Bridge St., Lyme Regis

Beatrix Potter (1866-1943), whose married name from 1913 was Mrs Helen Heelis, stayed for a fortnight at Burleigh Villas in 1906. While there she drew illustrations for *The Tale of Little Pig Robinson*. It was originally written in letter form in 1894 to a young relative, Eric Moore, and then subsequently published as her last book in 1930. It is noteworthy because the illustrations show the Cobb full of colliers.

Henry Handel Richardson (1870-1946) – the pen name of Ethel Florence Lindesay Richardson – wrote, in 1925, her novel *The Way Home*, which is set in Lyme. She lodged with Olga Roncoroni whose parents ran a tea-house and cinema in the Assembly Rooms, which moved to the old Bathhouse and Drill Hall (now the Marine Theatre) in 1928.

G. K. Chesterton (1874-1936) spent his holidays at the Three Cups in 1928, 1929 and 1930.

Ethel Mannin (1900-1984), a prolific author, wrote about A. S. Neill's Lyme school in her autobiography, *Confessions and Impressions,* published in 1930.[37]

John Fowles (1926–) still lives in Lyme and is the writer of many novels of which *The French Lieutenant's Woman*, published in 1969, is centred on Lyme. It opens: 'An easterly is the most disagreeable wind in Lyme Bay - Lyme Bay being that largest bite from the underside of England's outstretched south-western leg – and a person of curiosity could at once have deduced several strong probabilities about the pair who began to walk down the quay at Lyme Regis, the small but ancient eponym of the inbite, one incisively sharp and blustery morning in the late March of 1867.'[38]

Colin Dexter (1930–) published *The Way Through the Woods* in 1992. It is an Inspector Morse novel and part of it is set in Lyme at the Bay Hotel on the Marine Parade.

> ''Where are you thinking of?''
> ''Lyme Regis.''
> ''Ah. Glorious Devon.''
> ''Dorset, sir.''
> ''Next door, surely?''
> ''*Persuasion* – it's where some of the scenes in *Persuasion* are set.''
> ''Ah.'' Strange looked suitably blank.
> ''And *The French Lieutenant's Woman*.''[39]

Artists

Lyme was part of Lord Burleigh's Schematic Map of 1539. In the British Library, it appears to be the first known representation of the town.

Anthony Devis (1729-1817) exhibited at the Royal Academy and painted one or two watercolours of Lyme.

William Daniell (1769-1837) went on a painting trip from Land's End to Holyhead in 1813, and in 1822 went on a steamer from Sheerness to Torquay. On one of these tours, probably the latter, he painted the Charmouth shore.

George Cumberland (1754-1846) settled in Bristol, and painted Lyme in 1820.

J. M. W. Turner R.A. (1775-1851): his drawings of the town and the Cobb, painted in 1811, were included in the book *Picturesque Views of the Southern Coast of England.* He probably stayed at Providence Cottage in Sherborne Lane.

Thomas Girtin (1775-1802): his painting of Lyme is in the Mellon Collection at the Yale Centre of British Art, Connecticut, USA.

Samuel Palmer (1805-1881) drew the landslip in 1841 on a sketching tour of Devon and Cornwall.

James Abbott McNeill Whistler (1834-1903) was an American who worked mainly in England. He stayed at the Royal Lion for seven months in 1895 and took a studio at the back of 50 Broad Street where he painted town scenes, and a portrait of Rose Randall, the 'Little Rose of Lyme Regis', who was the daughter of Mayor G. H. Randall. He also painted a portrait of the Master Smith, Samuel Govier. Both of these paintings are now in the Museum of Modern Fine Art, Boston, Mass., USA.

Lucien Pissarro (1863-1944), the neo-impressionist son of Camille Pisarro, stayed at Fishpond near Charmouth and later moved to Heywood near Chard. He painted Lambert's Castle and other local beauty spots.

Paul Nash (1889-1946), an Official War Artist, took many photographs of Lyme.

Designers

The early settlement in Lyme was on either side of the river. As the town developed so this simple grid expanded. The river provided water, conveyed sewage, and had a path along the bank for ease of travel. It was easy to get to the sea, the boats, the fishing, and all your friends. The attraction of being in a community alongside the river grew stronger, so the number of houses increased, and the population multiplied. It became congested, fires often broke out, and disease spread quickly, but it was always a close settlement where the sense of belonging was strong. When the men went away to sea, the families that stayed at home were supportive of each other and cooperation between people, even when it only consisted of quarrelling and fighting, was total. Individualism was rare and loneliness even rarer.

The domestic architecture which accompanied this pattern of living consisted of basic hovels with no sanitation and with thatched roofs. The common 'land' was the sea; fishing replaced the animal rearing which was found just outside the town as well as in the rest of Dorset. Sadly, there are few remains of the dwellings which were at the heart of this early settlement.

The oldest building in town was the Parish Church of St Michael. It possibly started as a Saxon church and it is thought one of the windows in the tower may be of that vintage but the first recorded date is 1130. What is now the entry porch was previously the Norman nave. The building was consecrated in 1298 which was fourteen years after the first town Charter in 1284. This would have been just before the date of the building of the Cobb, the other man-made major architectural feature of the town.

The medieval square was in and round the houses at the bottom of the hill. This was also the heart of Tudor growth in the town and there are still vestiges of it in the Bell Cliff restaurant in Broad Street and the Tudor House on Church Street. Fires more than modern developments have caused the destruction of much of this fourteenth and fifteenth-century property.

The character of the heart of the town today is based on Georgian buildings, though some early Victorian houses have replaced the originals. Much of the main Broad Street is of this late eighteenth/early nineteenth-century period, and can be best appreciated if one looks above the shopfronts and the philistine decorations. Some of the houses were devastated by the 1844 fire, but there is still more than a sample of the fashionable town which was the seaside escape from Bath. Lyme attracted the famous like the Duchess of Kent and the Princess Victoria in 1833, Chatham and his son Pitt 'the Younger', Jane Austen and others who came regularly. Defoe called it a 'town of good figure.' One of the most interesting clusters of Georgian houses is in Monmouth Square which was between the peasant settlement around Coombe Street and Church Street. At this point, mention must be made of Thomas Hollis who bought the Three Cups hotel and persuaded many of the famous to visit it. One of the attractions was the Assembly Rooms where tea or coffee could be had every night for sixpence, twice a week there was card playing, and there was dancing on Friday nights. The house which is now the Alexandra hotel was built in 1735 and was originally the home of the Dowager Countess Poulett. She was the wife of Sir John Poulett, fourth Baron and first Earl (1663-1743). He was the grandson of Sir John Poulett who had been MP for Lyme in 1621-2, was a Cavalier, a Tory who had been First Lord of the Treasury and was made a Knight of the Garter in 1713. The house eventually passed to the Duc du Stacpoole and became a hotel in 1901. The Marine Parade, promenade, sea walk or whatever the fashion chose to call it at any particular time, was started as an up-market tourist attraction in 1760.

The Town Hall was rebuilt in 1887-8 on the site of the old Guildhall to commemorate the Golden Jubilee of Queen Victoria. At about the same time the Cannington Viaduct was started in Uplyme in 1903 and soon afterwards the Victoria hotel near the station. The purpose-built museum so recently restored in such a sensitive way was designed by the architect G. B. Vialls in 1903, financed by Thomas Philpott, and completed the following year.

At the Cobb end of town there are several nineteenth-century houses, a few cottages and the very precious inns which have survived the ravages of the weather. There is also a large bonded warehouse built in 1830 and now divided into flats. But the main building in this part of town, or indeed in Lyme as a whole, is the Cobb.

The first mention of the Cobb is in 1372 when a storm destroyed it and much of the town as well; but there is evidence that Lyme was a minor port earlier than this because it supplied a boat for 'use in the King's Navy' in 1293. However, once the Cobb was built trade came to Lyme as well as the need to defend the south-western shore against possible invaders. Storms often did damage to the original Cobb when it was made of wood and it was often completely destroyed or severely damaged. Grants were regularly given by the Crown, usually for major repairs, so that it would remain an important refuge for the Navy and for the essential trade with mainland Europe. When it was eventually constructed of stone it became less vulnerable although it has always needed regular repairs. It protrudes from the natural lie of the coastline and is therefore subject to the worst assaults of the sea.

There are some other buildings worthy of mention which give colour to the town. Belmont is an eighteenth century house decorated lavishly with coad stone, Coram Tower was built in 1903 as a theological college, and next to it is Coram Court built around 1887. Just above them is High Cliff House which was built around 1840 and was once the home of the Lister family. The group of cottages, including Madeira Cottage on the Marine Parade were all built in the first half of the nineteenth century. One of the joys of the town, though often obscured by heavy traffic, is the Tudor House on Church Street which is partly sixteenth century and partly eighteenth century, and still contains some of the original stone decoration and panelling from those periods. The Royal Lion in Broad Street was rebuilt after the fire of 1844. It is slightly pre-dated by the Three Cups which has a grander entrance of Doric columns.

The churches of the town are numerous. The Parish Church of St Michael is a mixture of several styles and contains fine memorials which reflect the nature of the port and the merchant venturers who used it. The next oldest building is the Baptish Church built in 1653 and always one of the major centres of Dissent in the town. The Congregational Church in Coombe Street was built in 1750-5 by John Whitty, Minister, architect and foreman. It is now the Dinosaur museum. The Methodist Church was situated below the Parish Church and was demolished to make way for flats. The Roman Catholic Church, designed by H. E. Goodridge in 1835-37, was built soon after

Catholic Emancipation. The adjacent presbytery was built to designs by Pugin although the original building has subsequently been modified. There is also the Peek Memorial Chapel which is adjacent to the Alexandra hotel and was built in 1884.

In the context of a chapter about the cultural life of the town, mention ought to be made of the Regent Cinema which was purpose-built in 1937 and is one of the finest small town cinemas in the country. It stayed open throughout the war and has an outstanding record of bringing new films to the town at the earliest opportunity.

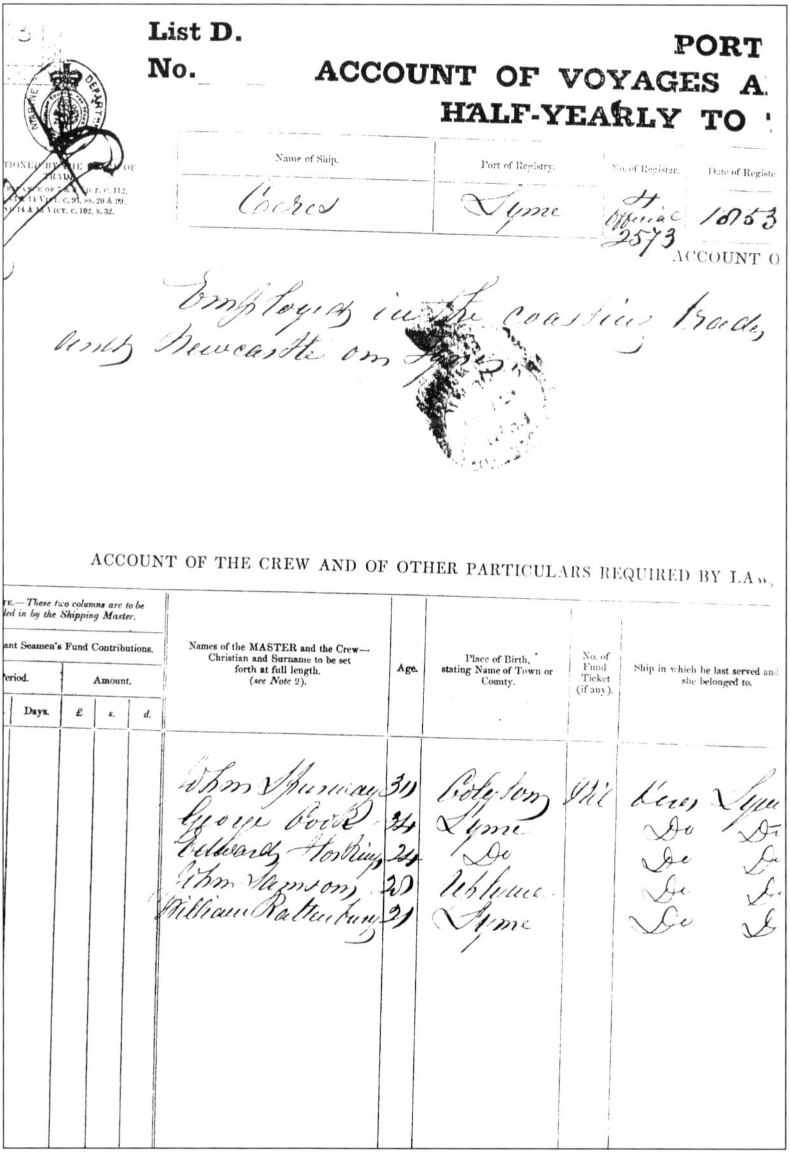

List D.

No.

PORT

ACCOUNT OF VOYAGES A

HALF-YEARLY TO

Name of Ship.	Port of Registry.	No. of Register.	Date of Registe
Ceres	Lyme	Official 2573	1853

ACCOUNT O

Employed in the coasting trade, unto Newcastle on Tyne

ACCOUNT OF THE CREW AND OF OTHER PARTICULARS REQUIRED BY LAW

...ant Seamen's Fund Contributions. Period. Days.	£	s.	d.	Names of the MASTER and the Crew—Christian and Surname to be set forth at full length. (see Note 2).	Age.	Place of Birth, stating Name of Town or County.	No. of Fund Ticket (if any).	Ship in which he last served and she belonged to.
				Wm Spurway	30	Colyton	Nil	Ceres Lyme
				George Cook	34	Lyme		Do Do
				Edward Hosking	24	Do		Do Do
				Wm Simpson	20	Uplyme		Do Do
				William Rattenbury	21	Lyme		Do Do

Extract from a ship's log plying the coal trade from Newcastle-on-Tyne to Lyme. The crew includes William Rattenbury, a familiar Lyme family

Granny's Teeth, early 1900s

Steamer coming into the Cobb

Marine Walk about 1870, showing the cart track from the Cobb to Cobb Gate

The Cobb, showing the Customs House

Bathing Caravans, 1870s

The Cobb with tennis courts in front

A photograph of 1939-45, one of the RAF launches, off the Cobb, with guns mounted. Copy given by Albert Brown.
I know of no other close shot of one of these launches

Lyme Regis Railway Station 1903, about the time of the opening

The Cobb, early 1900s

SS Victoria which plied between Weymouth and Torquay

Shipping in the Cobb, 1852-5

HMS Formidable

Funeral of those who perished on HMS Formidable. One of the coffins can be seen on the left

Masterman Hardy, the last sailing ship

Whistler's Studio on Broad Street

The Smith with Sam Govier, made famous by Whistler's painting

Victoria Hotel, the Railway Hotel

The three houses from left to right are:
1. The office in Wonderland Café, demolished after the subsidence of 1925
2. Tilings in 1925, pulled down in 1928
3. The balconies house called Cobb Cliff was pulled down in 1959

Late Victorian advert for the Royal Lion Hotel

The St Michael's Church School built in 1892

Lyme Regis Infants, 1926

RC Church of St George with the Presbytery just visible on the right

Cannington Viaduct with engines 30582 and 30583, 5 September 1959

Landslip, 1962

The Wesleyan Centenary Methodist Chapel, 1909

A meet at Hunters Lodge, 28 February 1899 (Gotley or Axe Vale)

A pigeon from the Wiscombe loft on Church Street

During the late war many pigeon fanciers voluntarily offered their own services and the use of their birds for special operations.

I wish to record my deep appreciation for the valuable services rendered by

R. Wiscombe Esq.

at a time of grave national danger.

J. J. Lawson

Secretary of State for War.

The War Office,
London,
December, 1945.

A national tribute to R.W. Wiscombe, the pigeon fancier of Lyme

THE

REGENT

LYME REGIS

Telephone - - - - - - - - 53

FOR YOUR INFORMATION

HOURS OF OPENING Nightly. Doors open 7.45. Commence, 8 p.m.
MATINEES WEDNESDAY AT 5 p.m. THURS. and SAT. at 3 p.m.

OCTOBER 11th WEEK ONLY.

PREMIERE PERFORMANCE MONDAY, OCTOBER 11th at 7.30 p.m. Doors open 6.45 p.m.

Two performances daily during the remainder of the week at 3 and 8 except on Wednesday. Wednesday at 5 and 8 p.m.

ADMISSION.

2/-, 1/6, 1/3, 9d. and 6d. 2/- and 1/6 seats bookable in advance. Box Office open daily 10 a.m. - 12.30 p.m., 2.30 - 4.30 p.m. and from 9 p.m. to 10 p.m. Children at reduced prices to all matinees.

ENQUIRIES.

Telephone Lyme Regis 53 for any information about the REGENT. Your enquiries will receive courteous attention.

CAR PARKING.

By courtesy of the Proprietor of the Alexandra Hotel (adjoining the REGENT) cars may be parked free of charge in the Hotel forecourt.

It is particularly requested that the minimum of noise is made by patrons using the car parking facilities.

PROGRAMME.

A copy of the REGENT programme will be posted free of charge each month to those patrons who leave their name and address at the Box Office.

A copy of one of the pages in the Souvenir Programme of the opening of The Regent Cinema, Lyme Regis on Monday, 11 Oct 1937 at 7.30pm. The opening ceremony was performed by His Worship the Mayor, The Rev G.F. Ayre JP

Shown on that night was The Gaumont British News and Hugh Wakefield in *The Jumping Man* and Robertson Hare in *Aren't Men Beasts?* Future Presentations included *San Francisco* with Clark Gable, Jeanette MacDonald and Spencer Tracey, *Romeo and Juliet* with Norman Shearer and Leslie Howard and *Our Relation* with Laurel and Hardy

CHAPTER NINE

MERCHANT ADVENTURERS

Some of those men who left the town to seek their fortune in far-off lands were very distinguished and all of them were brave. Some never returned to their home town and others came back as famous achievers. They went for a variety of reasons – poverty, religious freedom, duty, punishment, bereavement; but the consistent factor in all those who left was the spirit of adventure. The boats were small but in them men went across the high seas and landed in countries where their very lives were in jeopardy. As we consider their explorations almost as though they were a matter of routine, let us not forget their courage in going at all.

The merchant adventurers in Lyme were not a formal guild but a government-backed body of exporters who were trying to get a larger share of the wealth which followed from the voyages of discovery and colonisation. Discovery was linked with trade. Lyme had always been a centre for the export of wool, and it was the country district around the town which produced the raw material. By 1600 and until the seaside mania in the eighteenth century, Lyme ships were trading all over the Mediterranean and elsewhere to places like Africa, the West Indies and America.

Several key men led the way. John Cabot had sailed from Bristol in the spring of 1497 in the tiny ship *Matthew*, and possibly reached as far as Newfoundland. What was important for Lyme and most other west country ports was that the American fisheries soon replaced the more traditional Icelandic fishing grounds. We know that many Lyme fishermen fished the Newfoundland cod in the sixteenth century and continued to trade with the province well into the nineteenth century.

Admiral Sir George Somers was born in Broad Street on 24 April 1544, the third of five sons. His father, a merchant and Freeman of the Borough, was affluent, and rich enough to be considered suitable for George to marry Joan Heywood, the daughter of a yeoman farmer, in 1563. George went to sea when he was still a boy and was a member of several expeditions until his father and brother died. Then he returned to take over the family business. He soon escaped to sea again in 1595 when he was part of a privateering expedition to the northern coast of South America (the Spanish Main) and acquired enough riches to come home a wealthy man. He was MP for Lyme, was knighted and became Mayor. His last major venture was with the Virginia Company and he was the Admiral in charge of a fleet of nine ships formed to visit the colony. His ship, the *Sea Venture*, left Plymouth on 2 June 1609, but on 24 June there was a great storm and the ships in the flotilla were separated. The *Sea Venture* was wrecked and what was left finished on a reef on an island near the Bermudas. All aboard were saved, and within a year a new ship, the *Deliverance*, was built, the voyage was resumed and Virginia was reached. The Bermudas had first been discovered by Juan Bermudez of Spain but Sir George formally claimed them for King James I and left two members of the party to occupy the island until he could return several months later. Sir George died on 8 November 1610, the year after reaching Virginia. His heart is buried in Somers Gardens in St George, Bermuda, and his body was brought back to Lyme on 1 June 1611. The funeral took place on 4 June 1611 at the Church of St

Candida and the Holy Cross at Whitchurch Canonicorum. It has been suggested that Shakespeare was inspired by the Somers story when he wrote *The Tempest*.

A different kind of leadership was shown by Captain Sir Richard Spence who had entered the Navy at 14 and became Government Resident and Pioneer Farmer of the first British Settlement of Albany in the southern part of Western Australia. This consisted of about 20 houses established by a detachment of the Dorsetshire Regiment, the 39-54th Foot. Spence had gone there in 1833 and stayed until 1839 leaving his wife Anne (née Liddon) in their home at 6 Cobb Road. The colonisation of Western Australia had been encouraged by the glowing report on the area by Captain James Stirling in 1827. It was also accelerated by the fear that the French or Americans might move in first.

Others who sailed to seek their fortunes had less success than Somers or Spence. Two brothers for example, Sylvester Jourdain, a shipmate of Somers, and John Jourdain were both born in Lyme and were both sailor adventurers. John went to India and died there in 1619. Another local man called Larcombe was born in the town, went to New England in 1640, then returned to live in Tavistock where he died in 1669. The pulpit in Lyme Parish Church is the gift of Richard Harvey in 1613, 'one of the merchant adventurers of the town and also a London Merchant Adventurer', and the balcony at the west end commemorates John Hassard, another merchant adventurer, who 'built this to the glorye of Almightie God in the eighteenth year of his age Anno Domini 1611.'

Perhaps the most poignant stories are associated with the name of Thomas Coram (1668-1751) who was born in Coombe Street. His mother died when he was six and his father, a shipowner and shipwright, married again and went to London to set up a shipbuilding business where

Thomas was apprenticed at the age 11. Eventually Thomas became master of a vessel trading to the Colonies. He had the good idea of employing ex-Servicemen who had fought in the European wars and could find no employment in their own continent. The idea failed but it was an example of constructive forward thinking. He later became a shipbuilder at Dighton on the Taunton river in Massachusetts in 1604. When he sought to establish a Church of England parish in Taunton he was thwarted by the Puritans, but he did leave 59 acres of land that he owned in trust with the stipulation that it could be used when the inhabitants became more civilised. The land was sold and the proceeds were eventually spent on a library, and Coram persuaded the Speaker of the House of Commons to present a Prayer Book which it still cherishes. The Church at Taunton Massachusetts, was dedicated to St Thomas after Coram as well as the Apostle. A house on the glebe there was called Coram Hall. Coram returned to London and became a trustee for Georgia. He also helped to plan the colonisation of Nova Scotia in 1735.

He walked daily from Rotherhithe to the City and on his route he regularly saw unwanted and abandoned babies. Determined to do something about them he used his influence with important people like George Handel and William Hogarth to build the Foundling Hospital. The campaign, however, made him very poor although he lived to a ripe old age. He never returned to Lyme.

The failure of the Monmouth Rebellion, along with the recession, persuaded some of the residents to leave the country; some of them returned, so there was a regular coming and going of the disenchanted minority. This emigration bore little relationship to the much earlier Pilgrim Fathers who had sailed from Lincolnshire. The Lyme Dissenters were disgruntled rather than serious pioneers. These dissenting merchants, and others, included those who just wanted to trade with the New World. For example, the Tuckers and the Burridges traded as merchants and became MPs for Lyme. The Fowlers, the Courtneys, the Gundrys sought their fortune outside Lyme.

In 1719, the *Martha*, a merchant ship of 90 tons made a 65 day crossing from Lyme to New England with 24 men, women and children. One can only guess about the privations and deprivations which they experienced on that voyage and about life on the plantations when they landed. By the eighteenth century, trade in Lyme had collapsed, and most of the principal merchant venturers had left the town, or had given up their speculative businesses.

CHAPTER TEN

THE DEFENCE OF THE TOWN

Threatened by the Danes, plundered by the French, challenged by the Spanish, menaced by Napoleon, part of an anti-Nazi communication network involving messages carried by pigeons, Lyme has been, throughout its history, protected by the sea in all the attempts to defend itself or support the country. With all the expertise possessed by fishermen, Lyme provided an unofficial naval reserve because there were always trained sailors who could be called upon in times of crisis and need. The militia consisted of artillery who manned the batteries at Cobb Gate when it was necessary to repulse attacks from the sea. Even the RAF, when based in Lyme, restricted their efforts to an Air-Sea Rescue Unit. The only significant number of infantry troops stationed in the town were the Americans waiting to invade Normandy in 1944.

Lyme's official records of any connection with the sea start in 1214 when Lyme was included in a list of towns required to provide 'King's Ships.' This was later than other places situated between Southampton and Exeter probably because Lyme would have been a small port in those days with a few ships and a simple pier at Cobb Gate. The next mention is in 1234, during the reign of Henry III, with a writ ordering Lyme to stop any merchantmen sailing for French ports. This was not only a move to stop or reduce rampant privateering but it was also part of the growing anti-French feeling in England which had lost almost all of the French territories except Gascony. In 1265, the town needed defending from the attacking Dartmouth sailors against whom there had been serious fighting. A boat of 120 oars was ordered in the reign of Edward I for the Navy. In 1301 Lyme was ordered to send a vessel to carry the Earl of Ulster to help Edward I in his Scottish campaign. Of equal significance was the sending of four ships and 62 men to lay siege to Calais in 1343 in what was a crucial part of the Hundred Years War, because it gave England a vital port to which the English Troops could withdraw. The total number of ships in this fleet was 60 so the Lyme contribution of four ships was significant.

The time had come for Lyme to have its own more substantial harbour. The Cobb was first mentioned in 1372 when a storm had destroyed much of it and Edward III was asked for financial help including a lowering of taxes. He was asked again the next year because another storm had done even more damage to the town as well as the Cobb. It is likely that the first Cobb consisted of a simple wooden structure built on existing rock ledges, and it would have been very vulnerable in inclement conditions. In 1378 the Burgesses of Lyme petitioned that the town was being wasted by the sea and that the Cobb, which was then large enough 'to shelter 2 or 3 barges', had been destroyed in the gales of the previous November. Nevertheless in spite of the troubles which beset this man-made harbour, and although Lyme was always pleading poverty, there were more ships and trade was increasing. It seems that while the storms were savaging the Cobb, the Plague was doing the same to the local population so times were hard.

During the sixteenth century trade improved. In 1572, Thomas Colshill a surveyor of Customs, compiled a list of coastal traders of which Lyme had five of 20-50 tons and

10 of 20 tons and under. A comparable survey of the number of mariners at this time listed: 108 Mariners, 18 Ships' Masters and 80 Visiting Mariners, making a total of 206, which represented about 20% of the total population. Consequently when the Spanish threatened to attack there was a rich reserve of experienced mariners to call upon. In 1585 Philip II had seized all British ships in Spanish ports and these included the *Susan* of Lyme Regis. It was clear that the threat of a Spanish invasion was very real and it was feared that Lyme was a prime target. Hence a cannon was placed at the entrance to the harbour with enough men to defend the town.

In 1588, the Armada was sighted off Lyme and local people were able to watch the battle from the cliffs between the relatively small English fleet and the larger Spanish force. There were two Lyme ships in the battle, the *Jacob* (90 tons), and the *Revenge* (60 tons) which was commanded by Vice-Admiral Sir Francis Drake; the English fleet was commanded by Lord Admiral Howard who was on the *Ark Royal*. The *Revenge* was a three-master designed by Matthew Baker (1530-1613), a master-shipwright, who was responsible for the construction of more than 10 other ships, including the *Foresight* and the *Vanguard* and whose notes on ship design are in the Pepysian Library at Magdalene College, Cambridge. At least three other warships built in 1590 were all based on the design of the *Revenge*. They mark an interesting separation of roles between the ship designer ('molder') who in this case was Baker, and the men who actually built or 'framed' the ship who would be Lyme shipwrights in the case of the *Revenge*. It is noteworthy and impressive that the distinguished designer Baker should be satisfied with the level of skill and workmanship at the Lyme shipbuilding yard. It is also significant that the Lyme yard was prepared to forsake its usual practice of building by eye and making little use of a drawn plan. This must have been a remarkable change for the local men and says much for their humility and willingness to listen to new ideas. By this time Lyme had a successful and busy boatyard at the Cobb end of the town, which was able to make boats of the highest quality, some of them having a double function as both merchant vessels and, if necessary, fighting ships.

The Armada was eventually defeated off Gravelines in Holland, and the remnant was chased to the north of Scotland; eventually in 1591, there was a fight in the Azores between the *Revenge* and several ships of the Armada. Sir Walter Ralegh (1552-1618) comments in his report of the battle: 'The *Revenge* not able to move one way or the other, but as she was moved with the waves and billows of the sea commanded the master gunner, who he knew to be a most resolute man, to split and sink the ship; that thereby nothing might remain of glory or victory to the Spaniards.' Ralegh concluded: 'Many of the men were still alive to fight another day.'[40]

During the reign of Charles I the whole of the coast of the southwest was regularly marauded by large numbers of 'Mohammedan rovers' or Barbary pirates who had moved from the Mediterranean to the English Channel. The damage they inflicted on European commerce was hard to assess, but it was considerable and Lyme was not exempt. Locally they were called 'Turks' but they came from all over the Mediterranean and when sighted they were feared and dreaded. At this time the King's Navy had been neglected and so Charles raised a Ship Money fleet and Lyme was ordered to contribute £70. Although this tax was opposed by the town it did help to provide the money to retaliate against the pirates. In 1637 this naval fleet destroyed a number of the offending ships at Sallee which eased the threat to some degree, but the pirates were not really curbed until England, at a later stage, became a Mediterranean power by the occupation of Tangier and Gibraltar.

The next threat was more serious and came from the French in 1690. James II had escaped to France and was giving naval instructions in Brest as Louis XIV's navy sailed to fight the English. The French fleet of 110 ships in command of Admiral de Tourville fought the Battle of Beachy Head on 30 June 1690, reached Portland on 21 July, sailed past Lyme and on to Teignmouth which they sacked at 5pm on 26 July. They used 150 galleys manned by soldiers, slaves and convicts. Lyme must have had news of this, and when the French fleet arrived in Lyme Bay on 1 August 1690 the town was alarmed. The French threat was only five years after the landing of Monmouth. The severe punishments which Judge Jeffreys had meted out to the supporters made local people wary about another landing. The sight of the French navy made tangible the strained relations which had existed for several hundreds of years with the nearest foreign country. The French were not only Catholic and supporters of the Stuarts but they were also serious trading rivals in the Channel, especially of local trade. There was no love lost between Lyme sailors and their old opponents, so agitation in the town was very great about the possible arrival of the foreign fleet. The militia was quartered in the town, and a platform built on the Cobb on which guns were mounted; the other forts were on full alert with their 10 long 9-pounders. Watchers were posted night and day to look for possible attack. On 11 August one galley was sighted, having put out from the Admiral's ship. 'Several guns were fired at her from the forts but could not reach her; but from the Cliff (Gun Cliff) was fired a gun that did reach her, on which she went off to the westward.'[41] The tension was reduced at once with the disappearance of

Admiral Tourville but the whole event had been a real scare. Tourville himself thought Lyme 'will be very easy to sack and burn, ... is unfortified and as large as Orleans.' He was obviously misinformed because the town was fortified, and the French must have been surprised they encountered such overt resistance from the shore.

After the scare it was the turn of the French privateers to disturb the town, and the Lyme artillery felt it necessary to fire against them in 1705, 1744 and 1795. During these years there was also considerable anxiety that the supporters of Bonnie Prince Charlie might launch an invasion, particularly in 1745. This did not materialise, but there were fears that there might have been a version of the 1685 landing, only this time with Catholic supporters but with the same results of turmoil, punishment and social division.

From a military rather than from a strictly naval view, Lyme was distinctive. Most towns had a detachment of Independent Volunteers in the eighteenth century. These were independent of the government, which was not prepared to raise an army, and they even made their own uniforms. There were 13 southern coastal towns who tried in this way to be ready and prepared in case there was a possible Napoleonic invasion, but Lyme was not one of them and there were no Independent Volunteers west of Dorchester. *Ad hoc* groups of soldiers had existed in Lyme in the sixteenth and seventeenth centuries but none of them formed a regular force and they did not even justify the title of a private army.

Blackmore Vale and Sherborne were both successful in raising a detachment of local Yeomanry and they both had the advantage of having the necessary good supply of local horses, but Lyme was not so well served.

The militia was a form of conscription and every parish had to produce militia rolls. It would be unusual for all the names on the militia roll to be called upon but they could always be summoned in an emergency. There was no regular army stationed in Dorset in the early days, and therefore local recruitment, which always came easily when a town was near a garrison, was minimal here. The 11th Foot was raised by the Duke of Beaufort in 1685 to oppose Monmouth though it was recruited not in Dorset but in North Devon. The 39th Foot was raised in 1702 and provided the first troops in India, fighting successfully at Plassey in 1757, and a handful of the regiment did come from Lyme. The 54th Foot was formed in 1755 but recruited a further few from the town. It was the peripatetic Irishmen willing to travel anywhere who provided many of the recruits.[42]

Thomas Hardy in *The Trumpet Major* tells the story of the press-gang whose task it was to find recruits. They consisted of a body of soldiers under an officer who waited for homecoming fishing craft or other likely prey and 'pressed' or compelled men to take service.[43] Lyme had its full share of this barbaric and inhuman form of enlistment.

John Rattenbury, in his *Memoirs* published in 1837, writes 'Our country is called the land of liberty; we possess a just and invincible aversion to slavery at home and in our foreign countries, and it is triumphantly said that a slave cannot breathe in England. Yet how is this to be reconciled with the practice of tearing men from their weeping and afflicted families, and from the peaceable and useful pursuits of merchandise and commerce, and chaining them to a situation which is alike repugnant to their feelings and their principles? The impressed seaman in the day of battle may sacrifice his resentment on the altar of patriotism, or, inspired by the example of others, he may perform miracles of valour; but in the ordinary scenes in which he is engaged, he will find his duties intolerably irksome, and will be ready to seize any opportunity that may present itself of regaining liberty.'[44]

Lyme's first official volunteer unit, raised in 1860, was the First Hampshire Artillery Corps (Dorset Batteries) with headquarters in HM Dockyard Portsmouth. It was later reorganised as the First Dorset (Southern Division) Volunteer Corps Artillery, No 3 Company, Lyme Regis. The muster roll of 1877 included some familiar Lyme family names: Capt Richard Francis Hay, Sgt Major William Mansfield, QMS Henry Radford, Sgts Mark Lawton, Edwin Henry Wallis, Edward Foxwell, and 58 gunners which included Cox, Emmett, Govier, Paull and Street. Some of those same family names can be repeated on the war memorial rolls listing those who died in the world wars. The 1892 roll included Surgeon Lt Richard Bangay who was the local GP and also the first Medical Officer of Health to be appointed in Lyme, and two trumpeters, Ernest Camplin and Sidney Warren.

Lyme's own ship was HMS *Lyme Regis* and there were four who carried the town name. The first was built in Portsmouth in 1654, of 764 tons with guns, and named after the Siege of Lyme 1644. It sailed with Blake at Porto Farma in Tunis (1655), was in the blockade of Cadiz (1656) and in Stayner's Squadron with Blake at Santa Cruz (1657). In 1660 it was renamed the *Montagu* by the Royalists at the Restoration and took prizes of the *Pink* and the *Dogger* from Monmouth. The second was built in Plymouth in 1694-5, of 384 tons with 32 guns, and commissioned for convoy and cruising which it did with success particularly when it attacked and killed the pirate Blackbeard in Ocra Coke inlet in 1718 and took his ship. In 1720, after being rebuilt, it was lost at sea. The third was built in Dartford in 1748, of 587 tons with 24 guns, burned the *French Rose* at Malta, sailed with Boscawen's fleet at Gibraltar, and was wrecked in the Kattegat in 1760.

The last HMS *Lyme Regis* was a minesweeper of 345 tons with a maximum speed of 15½ knots. She was driven by a single turbine, which was unique in the Bangor class, and had accommodation for 76 men including 6 officers. She was completed in 1942 on the Clyde, served off Iceland and North Africa, and successfully led the Allies on to 'Sword Beach', Normandy, in June 1944 when the designated leader had been sunk. Town interest in the ship was considerable, and during 'Warships Week' in 1942 £45,528 was raised which represented £14.13s per head of population. This was larger than the £40,000 which had been raised in the previous year during 'War Weapons Week' for a motor torpedo boat. The increase in the amount of giving was possibly because of the local association with the ship. Lord Kindersley, President of the National Savings Committee, wrote to the Mayor: 'This special effort, resulting in the adoption of HMS *Lyme Regis*, will not only forge a closer link between the people of Lyme Regis and the Royal Navy, but it will also provide a lasting record of their patriotism.'

An official welcome was given to some of the ship's company in the Town Hall by Mayor Emmett. Commander Tidswell thanked Milly Frost, the daughter of CPO Frost, and the Brownies, for the welcome comforts they had knitted which were much appreciated. This visit was matched by a return to Devonport when the girls went on the milk train to get there on time. The White Ensign now hanging in the Parish Church was given to Milly Frost as a memento of the trip. While on the ship the sailors had damaged the Brownies' totem pole and the model of 'Brownie', so the ship's crew collected £15 to reimburse the Pack so they could replace the articles. The links with the ship were always close but no native of Lyme ever served on the ship. She finished the war without being sunk and was eventually used as target practice off Milford Haven, being finally broken up on 11 September 1948 at Sunderland.

At the outbreak of the 1939-45 war two 4.7 guns, disguised as a haystack, were installed by the Royal Artillery below the golf links and near to the present town football club pitch.

When the RAF came to Lyme it established an Air-Sea Rescue Station based on the westward side of the Cobb and a unit was stationed there from 1937 to 1964. The verbatim wording of the plaque on the former HQ reads: 'is dedicated to the Men of the Royal Air Force Sea Rescue Service who served at Lyme Regis with 37 Air Sea Rescue/ Marine Craft Unit (ASR/MCU) from 1937. Later became 111 Marine Craft Unit (MCU) until its closure in 1964. Among its Wartime Commanding Officers was Sir Algernon Guinness. They made sure, the sea did not have them. This Plaque Erected by the D. Day Aviation Museum. Chichester. Sussex.'

The permanent Royal Naval station was not a boat but a radar unit on Stonebarrow. They claimed to be the first of the Allies to spot the German battleships, *Scharnhorst* and *Gneisenau* as they were steaming along the English Channel on their way to the invasion of Denmark on 8 April 1940.

Lyme played an important part in the development of the National Pigeon Service which grew out of a sub-committee of the Committee of Imperial Defence. The pigeons were used by the RAF, the Army, and the Intelligence Services, and over 16,000 pigeons were sent with messages for dropping. The first successful use of pigeons was made in October 1940, and they provided agents with a means of communication for a particular purpose after they had been parachuted into enemy-occupied territory; but later the role was much wider. Osman in his book *Pigeons in World War* writes: 'Information, photographs, and diagrams conveyed by pigeon from enemy-occupied Europe were of immense value in the accurate location of German installations of vital importance, especially during the critical time when southeast England was being subjected to a perilously severe bombardment with new weapons.'[45] During the whole of the war, 7,556 reports of possible interest to the services had to be dealt with by the Air Ministry Pigeon Section. In 1945 a letter was sent to the Secretary of the National Pigeon Service Committee which said, 'The British Army, the RAF, and the Army of the United States have made fullest use of the pigeons supplied by the National Pigeon Service, and highly trained birds which have been lent by your members have also been employed in special missions and by the Resistance Movements of our Allies. Furthermore, the assistance of pigeon owners in carrying out the measures of control instituted in this country has been an important contribution to security.'

There is no precise record of the number of racing pigeons whose base was in Lyme Regis but there is a list of 38 birds from Lyme which achieved 'a meritorious performance.' Birds got on the list by being 'used on a particularly hazardous task since they were dropped by parachute in single bird containers into occupied territory in Europe with instructions to their finders to answer a questionnaire by means of a pigeon.' Many of the birds housed in the town were bred away from Dorset but some were raised in Lyme itself by G. Stoker and H. Sexton of Sherborne Lane and R. Wiscombe of 48 Church Street. The National Pigeon Station in Lyme was in the grounds of the High Cliff hotel.

The earliest mention of a Lyme lifeboat was when Captain Bennet, the coxswain, received a gold medal for his work in helping several craft which had been washed out to sea during a storm on 22 November 1824. The first death was when a coastguard member lost his life trying to save the cargo of the *William and Ann* in 1834. Between 1932 and 1937 and between 1964 and 1967, the station was manned by local sailors, and between 1937 and 1964 the emergency services were looked after by the RAF. The RNLI returned in 1967, mainly due to the efforts of Ken Gollop, with an Inshore Rescue Boat made of neoprene rubber which had been designed and tested by the headmaster and students of Atlantic College.

Today the work of the RNLI is done in conjunction with the daily helicopter coastal patrol and both are under the direction and control of the coastguard Service which has a unit in Lyme under the overall direction of the Coastguard Station at Portland.

During the war, the beach was covered with barbed wire, but some of this was removed when the Americans arrived in 1943. They were billeted all over the town. The Officers Mess was in what is now St Michael's hotel, but the Dorset, the Tudor and Little Park were all used, together with tented camps on the Sidmouth Road and among the trees on Timber Hill. They were armoured troops and drove around the town as though it was a garrison, but they did no damage except that it took longer to get into the cinema where queues were consistently longer than they have been at any other time. The American troops were preparing for D-Day and in June 1944 most of them sailed from Weymouth and Portland, with a few departing from Portsmouth and Southampton. A plaque on the wall of Woodville House in Silver Street recognises their stay: 'At this site Nov 1943 - June 1944 was located the headquarters of 'C' Co., 16th Inf. Reg., 1st U.S. Inf. Div. who led the assault landing at Omaha Beach on D-Day (June 6 1944) in Normandy,

France Capt. Victor H. Briggs C.O.' Many girls married visiting soldiers and emigrated to America.

Before the invasion of Normandy there was a simulated exercise, the Fabius, which took place on Slapton sands in Devon. It was disturbed by German surface torpedo craft and was described as a massacre. HMS *Saladin*, *Azalva* and *Onslow* steamed at full speed to the rescue, but 191 seamen and 441 soldiers were killed, which was more than would be killed on Utah Beach on D-Day. Most of the dead were washed ashore at the Portland end of Chesil Beach and it is surprising that there is no evidence of any being discovered at Lyme.

A wartime postcript from the autograph book of the Mostyn family kept during the first world war when Rhode Hill House was a military hospital and Woodroffe was the Commandant reads:

'I'm longing for my dear sweet nurse again
As I'm standing in the shell hole in the rain
I can hear her gentle laughing
As me she comes a straffing
Oh I'm longing for her sweet smile again

With best wishes to dear Nurse Mostyn for her kind attention to me during my sojourn at Rhode Hill Hospital from Private Fowler KOYLI (King's Own Yorkshire Light Infantry)

Wounded in the Somme Sep 3/16 (March 1916)
Wounded at Arras May 3/17 (March 1917)
Gassed at Ypres and been gassing ever since.'

ENDNOTES

1 W. Putnam, *Roman Dorset*, Dovecote Press, Wimborne 1984

2 F. J. Haverfield, 'The Romanization of Roman Britain', in Proceedings of the British Academy, vol. 2, 1905-62

3 *Domesday*, Aletco Historical Editions, Great Domesday, London 1986

4 Matthew Baker, "*Ancient-English Shipwrightry*", Fragments of manuscript (undated) in the Pepys Library, Magdalene College, Cambridge, and passim

5 *Armada, 1588-1988*, Penguin Books in association with the National Maritime Museum, London 1988. The official catalogue to the exhibition celebrating the four-hundredth anniversary of the Spanish Armada

6 M. Waltzer, *Revolution of the Saints: A Study of the Origin of Radical Politics*, Harvard 1965

7 G. Roberts, *The History of Lyme Regis*, Langton and Harke, London 1823

8 M. Ashley, *Cromwell's Generals*, Jonathan Cape, London 1954 page 118

9 A. Wood, *Memoirs of Queen Mary's Days*, Bodleian Library, Oxford 660c (21)

10 Dorset Record Office 171/1-2

11 Somerset Record Office T/PH/LRM/S1282

12 A. H. Edwards, *Who was Sampson Larke?* (privately printed 1990)

13 C. Wanklyn, *Lyme Leaflets*, Spottiswoode, London 1944 page 17

14 Dorset Record Office DVC/LR
15 Valerie Grosvenor Myer, *Obstinate Head, Jane Austen: a Biography*, Michael O'Mara, London 1997 page 108
16 John Fowles, *The French Lieutenant's Woman,* Jonathan Cape, London 1969 page 125 and passim
17 Jane Austen, *Persuasion*, World Classics OUP 1963 and passim
18 Dorset Record Office DVC/LR
19 Dennis Mills and Michael Edgar, 'The Nineteenth Century Censuses', draft of an article to be submitted to the Dorset Natural History and Archaeological Society Proceedings
20 Asa Briggs, *The Age of Improvement*, Longman, Harlow 1959
21 J. Murphy, *Dorset at War*, Dorset Publishing Company, Sherborne 1979
22 J. Lello, *HMS Lyme Regis*, Warships International, 1988
23 N. Tattersfield, *The Forgotten Trade*, London 1991 page 231
24 A comparable site at Elounda near Aghios Nikolaos on Crete was built by the Venetians and fed by a narrow canal through an isthmus. This enabled sea water to flood the pans and then evaporate leaving dried sea salt. The practice in Lyme could have been similar.
25 Shipping Register, 1869-94, HM Customs and Excise, Devon Record Office
26 G. Roberts, *The History of Lyme Regis,* Langton and Hawke, London 1823
27 C. Wanklyn, *Lyme Regis: A Retrospective*, London 1922
28 S. Bird, *Lyme Regis, Uplyme, and Charmouth Companion,* N. J. Clarke Publications, Lyme Regis 1985
29 Western Baptist Association Minute Book 1653 in the possession of the Kilmington Baptist Church

30 Dorset Record Office, Quaker Burial Ground 1822-49 NQ1
31 Joan Walker, *Child Mortality and Public Health in Lyme Regis*, Dorset Natural History and Archaeological Society Proceedings 1981
32 St Michael's School, Lyme Regis has some of the log books and Dorset Record Office has the rest
33 J. Croall, *Neill of Summerhill*, RKP London 1983
34 The Report of Lyme Regis and Charmouth Mechanics Institute in the Philpot Museum, Lyme Regis
35 Jane Austen, *Persuasion*, as in Note 17
36 Penelope Hughes-Hallett, *Jane Austen: My Dear Cassandra*, Collins and Brown, London 1990 page 50 and passim
37 Ethel Mannin, *Confessions and Impressions,* quoted in J. Croall, *Neill of Summerhill* (above) page 140
38 John Fowles, *The French Lieutenant's Woman*, as in Note 16
39 Colin Dexter, *The Way through the Woods*, Macmillan, London 1992 page 8
40 G. Hammond, *Selected Writings of Walter Ralegh*, Manchester 1984: 'Report of the Truth of the Fight about the Isles of Azores this last summer betwixt the Revenge one of her Majesty's Ships, and an Armada of the King of Spain'
41 C. Wanklyn, *Lyme Leaflets*, as in Note 13
42 The Military Museum in Dorchester has material about the First Hampshire Artillery and the First Dorset Artillery. The Dorset Record Office also contains militia enrolments.
43 Thomas Hardy, *The Trumpet Major*, Macmillan, London 1936 page 268
44 J. Rattenbury, *Memoirs of a Smuggler*, J. Harvey, Sidmouth and London 1837 page 16

45 W. H. Osman, *Pigeons in World War 2*, The Racing Pigeon Publishing Company Ltd., London 1950 page 2

PRIMARY SOURCES

DORSET RECORD OFFICE, Bridport Road, Dorchester DT1 1RP

The Lyme Regis Borough Archive. DC/LR. It contains Quarter Sessions, Hustings and Court, Coroner, Legal, Cobb, Sea-Walls and Shipping, Finance, Rates and Taxes, Charter, Deeds, Rentals, Elections, Charity, Wanklyniana

The Parish Church (the red book).
Register, Services, Incumbents, Churchwardens, PCC, Men's Society, Overseers of the Poor, Constable, Surveyor of the Highway

Archives consulted
List of Mayors 1285-1650 Pho665
Letter to Mayor of LR from Benzil Holles Pho184
Witchcraft. Examination of witnesses accusing Deanes Grimmerton of witchraft 1687 Pho173/1-5
Regulations of Lyme Regis Female Friendly Society 1794 DC/LR
Jordon of LR 1565-1613 went to Bermudas with Sir George Somers D574/96
Shipping Register MIC4 SR/L
Licence of William Hyett to redeem captive crew in Algeria
Logbooks of LR C of E School Boys 1863-1964 SI34
Plans of National School 1855 NG/ED/36

Orders to Keeper of Dorchester Gaol to take into Gaol LR inhabitants who supported Monmouth Rebellion 1685 Pho182

Press Warrants 1787 Pho 178

List of Dissenting Meeting Houses 1695-1721 Pho 183

Justices Pho 172

List of Inhabitants Pho 210

Gas Light and Coke Coy. 1835-1855 B2/4/1

Quaker Burial Ground 1622-49 NQ 1

Relief of sufferers after great fire 1844 PE/LR/SP1

Declaration of Mayor and inhabitants of abhorrence of 1745 Rebellion

Letter to George Trenchard concerning Bilton and Tucker Pho 177

Papists 1611 Pho 169

Letter to Sir John Stawell, Governor of Taunton from Charles I re the bringing of rebel town of Lyme to submission 11 Feb 1646 Pho 865

Info of Julian Marshall concerning Joane Brigs a thief 1688 Pho 174

Selected Militia enrolments for 1759, 1763-78, 1782

SOMERSET RECORD OFFICE, Obridge Road, Taunton TA2 7PU

Hewling. Memorial by Hannah concerning brothers William and Benjamin executed for association with Monmouth Rebellion. ND early 18th Cent. T/PH/LRM/S1282

DEVON RECORD OFFICE, Castle Street, Exeter EX4 3PU

HM Customs and Excise, Output of Exeter 3289S/12

Axminster Guardians Minute Book 1836-38

THE KEEP MILITARY MUSEUM, The Keep, Bridport Road, Dorchester DT1 1RN

Militia enrolments of First Dorset Artillery (Southern Division) Volunteer Corps Royal Artillery No 3 Company Lyme Regis. First Dorset Artillery Corps Lyme Regis

OXFORD BODLEIAN LIBRARY

Wood. Memoirs of Queen Mary's days 660c

BRITISH LIBRARY, Great Russell Street, WC1B 3DG

Linter Ricardo, various polkas, quadrilles, and waltzes 905.21 (Music)

List of names of rebels executed and those respited (Humanities and social sciences section)

Ordnance Survey Maps 1862 onwards (Map Library)

VICTORIA AND ALBERT MUSEUM, South Kensington, SW7 2RL

Three watercolours

John W. Abbott P6-1930, C. W. Bamfylde E343-1949, J. Hoppner P13-1925

ST MICHAEL'S SCHOOL, LYME REGIS

Various logbooks for boys, girls, infants

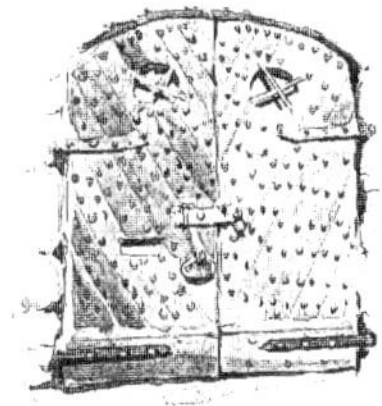

BIBLIOGRAPHY

M. Ashley, *Cromwell's Generals*, Jonathan Cape, London 1954

Thomas Coram mentioned in Parish Information booklet of St Thomas Episcopal Church, Taunton, Mass., USA 1992 Edition

R. Curle, *Mary Anning*, Dorset Worthies Pamphlet No 4, Dorset N. H. A. Society

J. Croall, *Neill of Summerhill*, RKP London 1983

Domesday, Aletco Historical Editions, Great Domesday, London 1986

A. H. Edwards, *Who was Sampson Larke?* (privately printed 1990)

A. Fagersten, *Place Names of Dorset*, Uppsala University Sweden 1933

J. Fowles, *A Short History of Lyme Regis*, Dovecote Press, Wimborne 1982

R. Hanbury, *The Grove*, a monthly magazine, Dunster, Lyme Regis 1891-2

J. Hutchins, *History of Dorset*, Third Edition, London 1861-74

Kelly's Directory of Dorsetshire, Wiltshire, Hampshire, London 1861

B. Kerr, *Bound to the Soil, A Social History of Dorset*, E. P. Publishing, Wakefield, West Yorkshire 1975

J. Lello, Article on HMS *Lyme Regis*, Warships International, Number 2 1986

L. Linder, *History of the Writing of Beatrix Potter*, Warne, London 1971

Lyme Regis Baptists, 1653-1953, privately printed pamphlet

V. G. Myer, *Obstinate Heart, Jane Austen*, Michael O'Mara, London 1997

J. Murphy, *Dorset at War*, Dorset Publishing Company, Sherborne 1979

J. Newman and N. Pevsner, *The Buildings of England - North Dorset*, Penguin. London 1972

J. Rattenbury, *Memoirs of a Smuggler*, J. Harvey, Sidmouth and London 1837

G. Roberts, *The History of Lyme Regis from the Earliest Period to the Present Day*, Langton and Harke, London 1823

P. Rogers, *Henry Fielding*, Paul Elek, London 1979

K. D. M. Snell, *Annals of the Labouring Poor*, CUP 1985

N. Tattersfield, *The Forgotten Trade*, London 1991

The Victoria History of the County of Dorset volumes 1 and 2, Constable, London 1908

E. P. Thompson, *The Making of the English Working Class*, Pelican 1968

C. Wanklyn, *Lyme Leaflets*, Spottiswoode, London 1944

C. Wanklyn, *Lyme Regis, A Retrospect*, Spottiswoode, London 1922 and 1927

INDEX

Air-Sea Rescue vii, 4, 34, 36, 38, 92, 100
Alexandra hotel 83
Alford Gregory 22, 56
Alfred 11
Allhallows School 74
Anning vi, 2, 6, 18, 30
Aragon 58
Armada 18, 39, 94, 95
Artillery 4, 97, 99
Assembly Rooms 4, 29, 30, 49, 83
Aulius Plautius 9
Austen 29, 30, 77
Axminster Union 4, 97, 99

Baker Matthew 18, 94
Bangay 63, 99
Baptists and Anabaptists 21, 23, 51, 55, 85
Barbary Pirates 95
Baucclеuch 6, 22
Beaminster 29, 72
Bermuda 88
Black Death 15, 59
Blake 21
Blue Lias 2
Brewery 48
Bridport 23, 72, 74
Britton vi
Buccaneers 19, 28

Calais 17
Caal verins 18
Cannington vii, 6
Case 65
Cement Works vi, 4
Charlemagne 14
Charles II 11, 21
Charmouth 9, 11, 49
Charters 8, 13, 44
Chatham 29, 83
Chesterton 80
Chideock 9
Cinema vii, 10, 86
Coade 26
Coal 48
Cobb vii, 1-4, 6, 8, 14, 17, 20, 23-26, 35, 36, 37-38, 45, 49, 84, 93, 95
Colshill 93
Colway Manor 13, 49
Copinger 40
Coram vi, 8
Coram Court 85
Coram Tower 85
Corruption 26, 27, 28, 29
Creeley 20
Cumberland 81
Customs House 38
Cynewulf 11

Dampier 31
Daniell 81
Danes 11, 12
Dassall Samuel 22
Deane 53
Defiance 41
Defoe 77
Devis 81

Devon Hotel 54
Dexter 80
Dissent and dissenters 19, 55
Domesday vi, 10, 12, 45
Dorchester 2, 3
Dorset 2, 12, 25, 28
Durotriges 9

Education 67
Edward I 13, 44, 93
Edward II 14
Edward III 14
Edward VI 45
Established Church 19, 51, 82, 85, 109
Eugenius 67
Europe 6, 28
Exeter 9, 10, 22, 26, 92

Fanes 26, 27, 28
Fee-farm 15, 17
Fielding 77
Fire 78, 83, 85
Fishing and fish days 17
Follett 28
Foundling Hospital 66, 90
Formidable vii, 8, 33
Fossils 1, 2
Fowles 29, 80
France 15, 16, 17, 25, 26, 28
Fuller 22
Fulling Tower vii, 12, 48

George I 28
Girtin 81
Glastonbury 13
Govier vii
Gneisenau 101
Granny's Teeth vii, 2
Green Hugh 19
Guildhall 4

Haverfield 10
Hawkins Jack 18
Health 59
Henley 30, 49
Henry II 13
Henry III 92
Henry V 17
Hewling William 23, 110
Hollis Thomas 29, 49, 83
Hundred Years' War 15, 16, 17, 93
Hunters Lodge vii, 8

Imperial Defence, Committee of 101
Infants School 6
Iron Age 9
Isabella 14
Isolationism 39

Jacob 94
James II 8, 22, 24, 25, 96
Jeffreys 23, 96
Jourdan 89
Jurassic 6

Kattegat 100
Kidd, John 23
Kindersley, Lord 100

Lace 47
Lambert's Castle 6, 9
Landslip vii, 1, 6, 30

Larke, Sampson 23, 112
Leprosy 59
Lifeboat 102
Lincoln 9, 22
Lister 66
London 8, 22, 23
Louis XIV 25
Lyme Bay 17
Lym River 4
Lyme Regis HMS 99, 100

Madders John 23
Malta 99
Mannin 80
Maps (1825) 4, (1841) 1, (1862) 2, Tudor 2
Marine Parade or Walk vii, 2, 3, 499
Marine Theatre 4
Marryat 78
Martha 91
Mary Tudor 51, 55, 111
Matthew 87
Matthews, Arthur 23
Maurice Prince 30
Mayor and Corporation 27, 28
Mechanics Institute 75
Melcombe 15, 16, 27
Merchant Guilds 14, 87
Methodists 56
Militia 97, 111
Mitford 78
Monkton Wyld 75
Monmouth 8, 21, 51, 56, 90, 110, 111
Monmouth Beach 2, 22
Montague Douglas Scotts vi, 6
Mostyn 104
MPs 14, 27
Municipal Reform Act 1835 31
Museum vi, 4

Napoleonic wars 26
Nash 82
Navigation Acts 29
Neill 74, 75
Nelson 26
Netherlands/Holland 25, 28
New England 89
Newfoundland 88
Normandy 35, 92, 100
Normans 12, 13, 82
North Africa 6
Nova Scotia 90

Ocra Coke 99
Oxford 21, 29

Palgrave 78
Palmer 81
Papist, popish 19
Parish Church 4
Parliament 13, 14, 15, 27, 28
Parliamentarians 19, 20
Peak 57
Pearn 71
Philip II 94
Philpot 84
Pigeons 8, 10, 101, 102
Pilgrim Fathers 90
Pilot Boat vii, 12, 34

Pinney vi, 8, 30
Piracy 40
Pissaro 81
Pitt 49
Plague 16, 93
Pollard, Sheila 10
Poole 12, 15
Poor Law 60, 61
Poor Rate 1681 4
Pope 59
Popham 21
Population 32
Potter, Beatrix 48, 79
Poulett 83
Privateers 26
Protestant 21, 22, 24, 25, 26
Prayer Book 90
Puritans 19, 20, 21, 51, 90

Quakers 56

Railway 6, 36, 41, 42
Ralegh 95
Rattenbury 1, 40, 46, 98
Rattus rattus 15
Raymond's Hill 9, 10
Reform Acts 14
Religious Development 6
Republican 24
Restoration 21
Revenge 18, 94, 95
Rhode Hill Hospital 104
Richard II 16, 17, 93
Richardson 79
RNLI 103
Roberts 67
Robins, Samuel 23
Roman Catholic Church vii, 6, 19, 52
Roman Lyme vi, 6, 9, 10, 11
Royal Lion 4, 14
Royalist 19, 20, 22
Russell, Richard 29

Salt 5, 15
Salisbury 12
Sampson Larke 23
Saxony 28
San Juan de Ulua 18
Scharnhorst 101
Scott, James 22
Scythe Men 22
Sea, importance of 6, 7, 8, 28
Sedgemoor 22
Seditious Lecturers 20
Seven Years War 28
Sewers 4, 65
Sherborne Abbey 11, 13, 44, 48, 53
Sherborne Lane 11, 53, 56, 64
Shipbuilding 17, 18, 19, 46, 94, 95
Ship Money 95
Short, Amos 54
Siege of Calais 16
Siege of Lyme 20
Sherborne 11, 97
Somers, George 88
Somerset 9, 21
Somerset Levels 11
South Cadbury 9
Southampton 92
Spanish Main 18, 28, 88

Spence Richard 89
Spittals 2
Stocks 1
Stokes, G. 102
Stone industry vi, 2
Stuarts 24
Summerhill 74
Sunderland 100
Susan 94
Swann 10
Sword Beach 100

Tapestry 57
Tattersfield 38
Taunton 21, 22, 23, 90
Taunton (Mass) 90
Teignmouth 96, 25
Tempest, The 89
Temple, Benjamin 23
Tennyson 78
Thomas, WH 71
Three Cups 29, 83
Tidswell 100
Tourism 29, 49
Tourville de vi, 8, 25, 96
Town Council 8, 27
Town Hall 84
Tuberculosis 65
Tucker, George 10, 91
Tudor Lyme 2, 18, 85
Turner 81
Tyler, Joseph 23
Typhoid 65

Ulster, Earl of 93
United States Army 35, 103
Uplyme 13
Uplyme Parish Church 54

Verbo Sacerdotis 22
Vialls 84
Victoria, Queen 33
Victoria, SS 6
Victorian 29
Virginia 88
Vienne 16
Volunteers 97

Walker 59, 63
Walters, Lucy 22
Walzer 19
Warships Week 100
War Weapons Week 100
Watton 71
Wedmore 11
Wesley 53
Wessex 11
Weston Zoyland 22
Weymouth 27
Whig 22, 26
Whistler vii, 1, 2, 81
William abd Ann 103
William of Orange 24, 25, 26
Wiltshire 11
Wings viii
Wiscombe R. viii, 102
Woodmead Halls 70
Wool trade 26
Woodroffe A.J. 69, 104
Wordsworth 77

Yeomanry 97